DRAWING *the*
GENERATIONS *Together*
to CHANGE *the* WORLD

CHILDREN, FAMILIES & GOD

LYNN ALEXANDER

DESTINY IMAGE™ EUROPE srl
Via Maiella, 1
66020 San Giovanni Teatino (Ch) – Italy

"Changing the World, One Book at a Time."

This book and all other Evangelista Media™ and Destiny Image™ Europe books are available at Christian bookstores and distributors worldwide.

To order products, or for any other correspondence:

EVANGELISTA MEDIA™ srl
Via della Scafa, 29/14
65013 Città Sant'Angelo (Pe) – Italy
Tel. +39 085 4716623 • Fax: +39 085 9090113
Email: info@evangelistamedia.com
Or reach us on the Internet: www.evangelistamedia.com

ISBN 13: 978-88-96727-72-0
ISBN 13 EBOOK: 978-88-96727-76-8

For Worldwide Distribution, Printed in Italy

1 2 3 4 5 6 / 15 14 13 12

DEDICATION

To my family of three generations. Your unwavering love for me has shaped me from my earliest days.

To all of the generations represented in Queens Park Baptist Church. For decades your desire to pursue God wholeheartedly has resulted in countless young people knowing a place of security, acceptance, and love. I was one of them.

Thank you both and all.

ACKNOWLEDGMENTS

This book would not be possible without some incredible people who chose to believe in me and the vision of this book—Peter and Angele Carruthers, Douglas and Betty Fergus, and Duncan and Kathy MacFadzean. Thank you more than you can know. Huge support for us as a family came from Brian and Vicky Allen, Steven and Helen Anderson, Kenny Borthwick, Niels and Alie Calvert, Ollie and Laura Clegg, Lorraine Darlow, Nick and Becky Drake, Edwin and Morag Gunn, Vicki and Jeff Hunt, Lorna MacDonald, Mark and Katy McKean, Keith and Donna Mack, Alan and Diane McWilliam, Ewen Peters, and Bonnie Yule-Kuehne.

Too many people to mention from the congregations of both Queens Park Baptist Church and Morningside Baptist Church took time to text, email, and write with encouragement and prayers for me—thank you all. So much of what I have written and experienced has been worked out in the safe place of these congregations. I hope you see things that will encourage you hugely in this book.

Grateful thanks are also due to the Baptist Union of Scotland for supporting my sabbatical time. I have deeply appreciated the time to read, write, and reflect on the past eight years of ministry. I also want to thank all those who played any part in my time studying theology at ICC, Glasgow (particularly my anonymous sponsor). Learning to reflect theologically gave impetus to this book.

Thank you to Allan Jack. If it weren't for you, this book wouldn't have been written. You encouraged me to step out of the boat big-time! James Glass—you have encouraged me in my writing from our earliest days of meeting; thank you for your wisdom and unfaltering encouragement to keep going.

Pam Lyall and family, thanks for the use of your "'office"'!'

"The three snowmen"—Revs. Kenny Borthwick, Ollie Clegg, and Ian MacDonald—and all the folks at Holy Trinity Church, thank you for loving our whole family and ministering so powerfully to us for these eight months. We will *never* forget our time with you.

Ashley Collishaw, Nick Jackson, Rich Johnson, Andy and Catherine Kennedy, Iain Macaulay, Alan McWilliam, and Judy White—thanks for giving me time and input and allowing me to share some of your stories in this book.

Mike Breen, Paul Maconochie, Rich Robinson, and all at Missional Communities UK/3DM—any "IRL" or online conversation I have had with you, any of your resources I have read or quoted from, are full of grace and with hearts that want to share fully with me all you have learned and practiced. Thank you.

Darrin and Daphne Clark in Catch The Fire Church, Toronto—your heart for children and their families as part of the mission of the whole Church has influenced and shaped me so much. I love what I see in you and your church.

Thank you to all at the Barna Organization, and in particular to George Barna and David Kinnaman, for the information you provide people like me and for the grace with which you share it and the heart you have to serve and support us in the church.

An additional thank you to the lovely Niels and Alie Calvert of Blue Sky Photography, who produced my photograph and promotional DVD for this book.

Massive thanks to the group who helped to edit me—not an easy task! I took up a lot of your time—Steven Anderson, Kenny Borthwick, Dr. Mark Elliot, Edwin Gunn, and Rich Robinson. Steven and Edwin get medals for doing the whole lot!

To those who wrote recommendations for this book—thank you for the investment of your time to read my scribblings one dark, cold January.

Thanks to Pietro, Berhanu, Marzia, and all at Evangelista Media (formerly Destiny Image Europe) who encouraged me all the way and who received this manuscript with real favor.

Finally, my husband, Scott, and my precious children, Evie and Joel, have been so patient and kind in these months and truly ran alongside me with the vision for this book, cheering me on 24/7. I love you so much, and you truly do provide the safest place for me to practice what I preach—we're all in it together! Thank you so much.

ENDORSEMENTS

Page after page of this excellent book is filled with the testimonies of children, young people, and families who have been completely transformed by the love and power of God. These stories are woven together to produce a passionate and articulate advocacy for the Church to move in a new way. Lynn is calling on the Church to embrace whole family discipleship and so much more. This is a radical departure from a great deal of what is currently happening in children's, youth, and family work within the organization of the church.

I believe that this is a prophetic book—there is something here that is a foretelling of what the Lord wants to do in our nation. Lynn boldly lays out a way of thinking and being the Church that will enable every generation to find their place within the Church's new awakening. I strongly recommend the reader to take time to read, ponder, and weigh what is being said here. There is a way ahead within these pages.

Alan McWilliam, Church Leader
Whiteinch Church of Scotland
Chairman, CLAN (New Wine Scotland)

In this book, Lynn clearly guides you through the maze of different ideas and thoughts regarding children and God, using the Bible, others' revelations, as well as her own experiences, to bring you to a place where, I'm convinced, your spirit will find an excitement about the possibilities which lie before us.

This is a book not only for children's pastors and children's ministry volunteers. It is also not directed to senior pastors (although every one of them should read it...and process it!); neither is it a parenting book. It's a book about spirituality, yet it skillfully weaves in practical ideas which we can embrace, as we facilitate environments for God to be God, in our children.

If you're already sold out to loving and raising children spiritually, this book will encourage you. If you have children but are neutral on spirituality, it will ignite an urgency within you; and even if you have no involvement with children, you will learn how to pray.

If you believe that the Bride of Christ is made up of every generation, this book is a must!

Enjoy...and be blessed!

Darrin and Daphne Clark, Children's Pastors
Catch The Fire, Toronto, Canada
Missionaries, Mercy Mandate

In this book, Lynn Alexander provides much-needed insights and challenges for the Church if we are to effectively engage in mission that sees whole households come to faith and children come into their full potential in the life of our churches.

This book is thoroughly biblical and very well-researched providing many excellent insights on areas of faith and family especially. Lynn doesn't hold back any punches but presents the reader with lots of challenges and searching questions that need to be asked in this thought-provoking work. Yet at the same time, Lynn serves up an abundance of helpful and practical ideas and suggestions which come from her own years of experience—experience that has born good fruit and enabled her to work through some tough questions and find some answers that can point us in a good direction.

Steven Anderson, Director
Healing Rooms Scotland

This book is a must for all who are involved in work with children and families. Lynn writes to us in a compelling, passionate, and ultimately prophetic way as she challenges us all to pay attention to how we can better help children and families encounter Christ, and then go on to be discipled. With a deep understanding of the spirituality of children, the image of God that they carry within them, and the need for the Church to reconsider how best to awaken and bring to fruition the spirituality of children, this is a must-read for all who want to see the miracle of new life in children and families and in local churches.

Mark Bailey, Lead Pastor, Trinity Cheltenham
Regional Director, New Wine Network

If the things that Lynn is saying are true, then as a pastor I am both comforted and challenged as I think of the possible shape of church to come. I happen to be convinced that what you will read in the following pages is indeed true, for its main themes accurately reflect the Scripture's teaching about the spirituality of children. Thirty years of pastoral experience and more years than that of reading the Bible have convinced me that Lynn places her feet in the right starting blocks in this fast-paced and energetically researched book as she poses the question, "Do you believe children are born with an ability to connect with God?"

This book not only examines that question but allows it to search church life and practice. It is precisely this searchlight quality of truth that comes from God that brings both the comfort and the challenge. Please receive both fully as they come to you from the heart of someone, who more than most people I know, carries the heart of God for both children and the Church. Read it and respond to it with the help of God's Spirit, for I believe it is with the help of God's Spirit that it has been written.

Rev. Kenny Borthwick, Holy Trinity Church of Scotland
Wester Hailes, Edinburgh

Lynn Alexander writes with the same infectious passion that she exhibits throughout her ministry. This is a book that will both challenge and move you. It has its foundation in robust theological and biblical reflection and builds on that to bring our practice under scrutiny. It draws on the best thinking about ministry with children and families, and also throws fresh light on a biblical understanding of family and community. Throughout, Lynn is able to illuminate the principles from her own experience, using real life examples of children and families coming to know and experience God.

And it is here that the book brings its greatest challenge—can we help children not just to be informed about God, but to experience Him and serve Him? And in the process, this will not be one-way traffic; we have much to learn from children and their trusting response to their heavenly Father. Here is a book that calls us to review our attitudes and our practice, which makes the book a less than comfortable read. But there is not just critique; this book is full of helpful guidance. We have much to thank Lynn for in producing such a stimulating, practical, and envisioning work.

Andy Bathgate, Chief Executive
Scripture Union Scotland

This book will impact you. I have known Lynn for all of her Christian life and have seen the Lord lead her and work through her in powerful ways. Most of all I have been challenged by her enthusiastic passion for Jesus, her absolute conviction about children's spirituality, and her desire to see genuine intergenerational community being lived out in the Church in the West today.

This is not a quiet book about theories of working with children, although there is a lot of research and plenty of practical help. Rather, its truths have been hammered out on the anvil of experience of working with children, parents, and other leaders. As a pastor of many years, I wish I had seen it a long time ago. Parts of it have challenged me profoundly, and I believe you will be challenged too. Most of all, you will be encouraged to help the Church "get ready" for what is to come.

Rev. Edwin H Gunn, retired Senior Pastor
Queens Park Baptist Church, Glasgow

Occasionally, a book comes along that combines insight, information, and inspiration. This title by Lynn Alexander is such a book. It is written in a very accessible style that at the same time does not compromise on scholarship. Lynn somehow manages to set out her case in a manner that is both reasonable and inspirational. Personal stories are blended with serious theology and practical application to produce a prophetic take on the state of children's and family ministry today and outline some potential ways forward for the future. There is so much good material within these pages; the book is worth buying just for the chapters entitled "Families in the Old Testament" and "Families in the New Testament." Lynn has done the whole Church a real service with her work. Buy the book—but be warned, you might want to work with children when you've finished reading it!

James Glass, Senior Minister
Glasgow Elim Church

As we have worked with many churches to help them develop a discipleship culture, we have found that children are often treated as an afterthought. In this excellent book, Lynn brings a timely challenge to put young people at the center of life-on-life communities reaching out to others. This is an important book, and I believe it is an authentic message from God to our generation.

Rev. Canon Paul Maconochie
Baptist Minister and Senior Team Leader
Network Church Sheffield

As the mother of a young child, I am thrilled to see Lynn's compelling thoughts on children's spirituality and the faith journey that children and adults can go on together. This is an insightful and practical book.

Bonnie Yule-Kuehne
UK Development Director
Alpha International

TABLE OF CONTENTS

INTRODUCTION

This book is written because of a longing in my heart that has grown and grown as the years have gone past. Put simply, I am writing this book because I believe the time is coming when children and their parents are going to come to faith and present themselves in our churches in great numbers. They will come from backgrounds where no one in their families will know anything of the stories of Jesus. We are already in days where most of us meet children and teenagers with parents and grandparents who have never attended church and have a very low opinion of the Christian faith, due to things they have heard or seen. Jesus, as you might know, for many people is truly on par with Santa and the Easter Bunny...or simply a swear word.

I became a Children and Family Pastor because God pulled me into it. My family and I had not been going to church since I had attended during the early Sunday school years. But then at age 14, I talked with a Christian girl at a wild party, and she invited me to her baptismal service. There I fell in love with the Jesus I saw demonstrated to me by the scores of teenagers around me. Weeks later, I had a powerful encounter with the Holy Spirit who filled me to overflowing. I became excited about all the possibilities that this "life in all its fullness" held, in a way that I continually come back to again and again. I ran after all that He had as fast as I could.

I've been involved in church leadership since my late teens and later became heavily involved in pastoral care and discipleship of teens and young adults. I also became the Area Leader for several small groups. I served gladly in one of the worship bands, and no matter what setting I was in, alone or with others, I loved pursuing the presence of God and leading others in the same. To this day, this remains one of my greatest passions.

To complete this picture, I taught in a state school as a secondary school teacher, working with 11 to 18 years old.

But all this changed when in 2003, I clearly heard God say, "I'm calling you to work with younger children." The journey I have been on since would take up hundreds of pages. I want to allow some of that journey to be revealed as you read on.

This book is not intended to be a complete definitive manual of "how to's" nor a succinct summary of every theological writing on children and family. I have, however, deliberately intended it to be a little of both, trusting the Spirit of God with what I believe He has said to me thus far—to excite and challenge you as church leaders, pastors, ministers, parents, and children's workers *for that which is ahead.*

In Second Kings 3:16, the Lord tells Elisha to make the valley full of ditches (NKJV). He will not see the wind or the rain come down; yet the ditches will be filled with water, and he and his cattle will drink. It will be a sovereign act of the Lord Almighty.

So if you lead a church that is longing to make an impact on this world, it's time to get the ditches ready, to prepare the structures for what is ahead. I believe we will see again the transformation of society that is inextricably linked to the transformation of family life. Children will lead their parents and vice versa. The Church is in desperate need of advice and guidance on how to nurture children's spirituality and not to ignore or destroy it, in order that these young ones would go further than we have ever gone before. And speaking as a church leader in the "sophisticated" United Kingdom, we are in desperate need of any intervention from God that will stop the "exodus" of children and young people from our churches.

In addition, I sense it is time for compartmentalizing to cease; seeing children's ministry as something that happens "over there" with its own branch of theology, with its own "how to" books, with its own language and culture. I feel as if God has called me to pull down the partitions which we have constructed for our own ease and convenience. There will be times where we meet physically all together, and there will be times when children, teenagers, and adults spend time separately; but there is coming again upon the Church a re-visiting of what it means to be generations together praising Jesus, learning from Him, and impacting the world significantly. Generational differences are intentional so that the impact of the generations together would send a powerful message.

Returning to Second Kings chapter 3, notice that in verse 20, the ditches were filled with water the next morning, just as the Lord had said would happen. But when did the water come? In the night? In the twinkling of an eye? or…?

We may not see any signs of what is coming; nevertheless, let's make ready.

Lynn Alexander
Edinburgh, Scotland

PART I

PREPARATION

Chapter One

CHILDREN'S SPIRITUALITY AND FAITH DEVELOPMENT

At Easter time in 2011, two small boys, age seven and eight, visited a church's 24/7 prayer room together. They attended a kids' midweek club run by the church and tended to attract trouble. On this day, they stayed in the prayer room for hours, alternating between lying quiet and still, and drawing images of Easter, like the cross and the grave. Thinking they had been in the prayer room for rather a long time, the pastor of the church asked them to take a break and go outside and play football. Meanwhile, two teenagers went in to pray. When the young boys saw them go in, they started to chant, "We want to pray! We want to pray!" So the pastor allowed them to return to the room.

The hunger of these two young boys (who do not routinely attend church), to pray and be in God's presence, seems inexplicable.

A mother of a five-year-old girl, who had just started school, had coffee with me. Knowing my job as a children's and family pastor, she asked if I could explain to her why her daughter was asking about Jesus on the cross. Mom was asking me how one so young could be asking these questions. She explained that she was attempting to raise her daughter in a spiritual vacuum "so she could make her own mind up about matters of faith"; moreover, they owned no Bibles. She was certain she had not seen any religious imagery showing Christ on the cross. School had been in session for only a matter of weeks, and she knew there had been no religious education presented, nor was it Easter or Christmas time. It

23

was a non-denominational (secular) school, and there had been no assemblies. What had given rise to these questions?

These two stories from Western culture demonstrate the urgency with which I write this first chapter. *Children are spiritual beings.* And increasingly in our sophisticated culture, they are asking spiritual questions. Parents, in their desire to connect with their children and be better parents, are listening to them, perhaps in ways that previous generations had not.

And when parents are not listening to them, or as the second story shows, don't want them to hear about Jesus—God is revealing Himself to children.

I have come across the following research carried out by a major secular publisher of children's books. Dorling Kindersley asked 1,500 parents and children age eight to twelve to provide their top 20 unanswerable questions. The top ten questions included: *"Does God exist?" "Is there life after death?" "If God made us, who made God?" "What does God look like?" "Why is the world here?" "Why are people bad to each other?" "Why are we here?"*[1]

These high-order questions are being asked by children under 12 to their parents who want to be able to answer them, but are struggling to know how to.

We have the answers! I write this book to prepare the Church, to issue the call to "make ready." This will mean a change in the way we "do church," as we in the West can't seem to be able to hold on to the children and young people that were ours at one time.

Consider part of the prophecy of Jean Darnell given in 1987.

> The second thing is that the Lord is going to send a tremendous revelation of Himself to boys and girls in this country. Between the ages of nine and fifteen particularly, children will begin to have a revelation of Jesus. They will see Him, they will know Him, they will hear Him, He will speak to them. He will come to them in visions and dreams; He will reveal His word to them. They will be converted and filled with the Holy Spirit and gifted by Him. And they will start praying. They will be healed themselves, and they will start praying for each other; and there will be wonderful healings through these boys and girls.

They will not only be the children of Christian parents. The Lord is going to manifest Himself to those who are in non-Christian homes where there is no love nor real family unity, where there is no knowledge of the Lord at all: perhaps not only for one generation but for many generations no Christian person has been in that family. But Jesus is going to meet them and reveal His power and His presence to them and His love for them. When they start coming to our children and to our teachers and telling what they are seeing and hearing from the Lord, our duty will be to receive them and love them as they are—because they will be rough diamonds, and they will have rather unusual, un-churchy language. But their experiences will be real. Some of their experiences will be so unusual you may doubt them. At that point receive their testimonies at face value, give them the word of God, and teach them how to love: because these children will have ministries not only as children, but as leaders in their adult life, and they will bless your country and other countries. So receive these children, teach them. Those of you who teach Sunday school, those of you who have children in your home and neighbourhood whom you are concerned about, begin to ask the Lord to raise your level of expectation of what they can receive, because they are going to start hearing. And just like the adults, they will start hearing the word and receiving the Lord and being able to receive deep spiritual experiences in the Lord.[2]

Children are made in the image of God. They possess this God-shaped yearning and longing and seem to connect very easily with Him. Given any and every opportunity, something seems to awaken.

I could fill the pages of this chapter with comments from parents of young children in the communities outside of our church walls. Here are just some of the questions I have heard:

- My child wants to pray. What should I do?

- My child is asking me about the Christmas story. How can I explain it?

- My child says she has have seen an angel. Should I believe her?

As you read these questions, ask yourself, "Has anyone outside of the church asked me those questions? How did I answer them? How confident did I feel about the answer I gave?"

If you or your church have had limited opportunities to engage in an open dialogue with parents or teachers and their children's spirituality, hang on to your seats, for I believe God wants to take us into these realms where we engage with children and families in bold, brave new ways. I am convinced that this is the time for the church to move away from a "come to us" model, and particularly in the realm of young people and their families where doing what we have always done is simply not cutting it anymore. More about that in later chapters!

The starting point is our understanding of children's spirituality. This book will attempt to stir you and encourage you and your church to engage with this awakening awareness of spirituality—no longer the realm of New Agers but now also the realm of intuitive parents. This is a period like no other of open doors, where children are gazing up with awe and wonder to the Maker of the stars, to the One who gave them breath. Their parents are looking to someone for answers to the questions their children pose—and the Church of Jesus Christ is positioned in the ideal place to do so, if only we would awaken to the innate desire children have to connect at a deep level with God their Father.

What Is "Children's Spirituality"?

It's really important to think about our own perspective and experience as we consider the spirituality of children. Are we afraid of the word "spirituality"? Does it conjure up images of Eastern meditation or New Age practices? Some important work has been accomplished in the worlds of theology, psychology, and educational theory, and I would like to point you toward some important Christian work on children and spirituality. Please hang in there with me, as I hope to illustrate that, far from being a threatening New Age concept, spirituality is something every one of us is born with, a desire for a connection with someone or something *other than ourselves*. As Christian leaders, it is vitally important that we be poised to introduce the man, woman, or child to the incredible person of Jesus in whom all longings for relationship are met.

Dr. Rebecca Nye suggests a very simple definition of children's spirituality:

God's ways of being with children and children's ways of being with God.[3]

She adds:

> ...this definition helps us to remember that children's spirituality starts with God—it is not something adults have to initiate. God and children have ways of being together because this is how God created them.[3]

I have worked as a pastor and adviser for many years now to churches of differing denominational backgrounds. I have found the following two questions to be the most pivotal in determining how churches will move forward in their ministry to children:

- Do you believe children are born with an ability to connect with God?

Even more than that...

- Do you believe children, who have no connection with church nor any relative who follows Jesus, who may not have a single person praying for them, have an ability to connect with God? Do you believe they may have already experienced something of a connection with God?

This is an incredibly helpful starting place for you, as the reader of this book, to audit your own views on how you see children.

For too long, we have treated children as empty vessels needing filled with our input. Even the most common description for those who work with children—Sunday School "teacher"—indicates that we, the church, have to impart *our* knowledge and experience to children. Without us, it could be presumed, they are spiritually ignorant, empty of knowledge, and scant in experience. They need "us."

However, several studies have proved that spirituality is a common and natural feature in children's lives. And there doesn't appear to be a type of child for whom this isn't the case.[4]

Academic research seems to go hand in hand with a theological understanding of *imago dei*. Imago dei is the assertion that humans are created in the image of God; therefore, there are special qualities in human nature which allow God to be seen in and interact with humans. Put very simply, we can see elements of God's nature in a person (child); and we are "wired" to connect with God because He has designed humans to do so.

The *New Scientist* magazine carried an article in its February 2009 edition entitled "Natural Born Believers."[5] Paul Bloom, a psychologist at Yale University says: "There is now a lot of evidence that some of the foundations of our religious beliefs are hard-wired." The article goes on to quote anthropologist Justin Barrett of Oxford University who states that: "Children the world over have a strong natural receptivity to believing in gods because of the way their minds work, and this early developing receptivity continues to anchor our intuitive thinking throughout life." This sentence substantiates Dr. Nye's assertion that children do not need adults to kick-start their spirituality.

Richard Dawkins is also quoted in this article as saying, "I am thoroughly happy with believing that children are predisposed to believe in invisible gods—I always was." His concern has always been that Christian parents/workers propagate religion through indoctrination; whereas, I would put forward that we nurture something that is already placed there by God from the beginning of creation. We were made for relationship with God—Ecclesiastes 3:11 (in most translations) describes the longing and yearning of the human heart to connect in this way: "He has also set eternity in the human heart."

But the real punch is in the closing paragraph of this article. Academics are wondering whether there is more to this hard-wiring than they even thought possible. Could there be definite proof that there is something supernatural at work? If children were left to their own devices, with no input from anyone else, raised in isolation, would they be able to create their own "religious beliefs"? Psychologist Bloom says that he thinks the answer is "yes." And I think he is right.

HOW DO WE GROW SPIRITUALITY INTO FAITH?

This next section raises an important question for pastors, church leaders, and parents. You can answer this question only if you know what the children in your church and families are being taught. What happens when they are not with you? What are children learning and experiencing of God when you're not there?

Consider the following:

- Is spirituality being nurtured in your ministry to children *in the church* and to children *outside the church*? (Remember both groups of children possess spirituality, not just the church kids.)

- Are children allowed to talk things over and ask questions? Or are they talked at?

- Is learning in the form of catechism, by rote, all about "head knowledge"?

- Are there opportunities to feel, to think and reflect, or to do?

- Are Bible stories repetitive and rushed, or is there time to put yourself into the story, imagining how it would feel if you were there?

- Are children given the opportunity to emotionally engage with the stories of the Bible?

- Are children given opportunities to respond to God?

- What does that look like? Is it programmatic ("bow your heads and pray after me…"), or are times of response varied and spontaneous?

This list of questions can be very challenging for many church leaders in the rich Western World, not just when teaching children but when educating adults too! We have developed a system of complex partitioning in church life—adults are taught *here*, young people are taught *there*, and children are taught *over there,* and occasionally (or never) there will be mixing. I do applaud the move to appoint children's and youth specialists on church staff. For reasons that I won't go into here, the real danger is that in the act of doing a good thing, senior pastors, elders, or church boards consider this area of ministry "covered"; in other words, leave it to the specialist staff member and concentrate on the "important business" of ministering to adults.

In these days when many people feel a longing for something more, I believe there is a need for a wake-up call to the Church to embrace the young who are desperately in need of spiritual nurture which will lead on to spiritual activation. And spiritually active children can then revolutionize those who come into contact with them. Not only that, but they become spiritually active adults who know what it is to respond to God and minister in power with a sense of their identity and inheritance.

Is it just possible that we might not see the harvest we long for, until we nail the ability to nurture the gift of children that has already been given to the Church? That role belongs to us as parents, grandparents, aunts, uncles, brothers, and sisters? It is unfortunate that we be so intent on our own empowering and transforming by the Holy Spirit and a desperate desire to reach those outside the church that we neglect the ones who are in our own arms and in our childcare and youth programs? Later in this book, there will be an opportunity to address these kinds of heart issues, where there has not been a deliberate intention to miss this chance; but nevertheless, it has happened.

There are some very practical steps that can be taken to help support a growth in children's spirituality. If you are a senior pastor looking for a resource for your staff or elders to read and discuss together, do check out Rebecca Nye's chapters[6] on this topic.

I want now to address the thorny question of children and conversion.

THOUGHTS ON A CHILD'S CONVERSION

Readers may find the notion of a child's spirituality a "fuzzy" one; and depending on the context you live and work in, and your theological background, you might well be looking right now for the answer to the question, *"When is a child definitely a Christian?"*

We have already looked at children's innate ability to connect with God. Hold this in mind as you think of children who are not yet part of any church, who, at this moment are playing with toys at home, or in a school halfway across the country, or are involved in subsistence farming somewhere far, far from you. Are they thinking of their Creator right now? How does He see them? I once heard someone say to a friend that their child wasn't *"quite there yet"* in regards to the child's commitment to Jesus—when I knew that child to be worshipping Jesus, a real prayer, and engaging avidly with the Bible. What they meant was, that as far as they knew, their child had not said "the sinner's prayer." Is this the only way we measure spirituality? Although somewhat controversial, I must ask, did Paul say the sinner's prayer on his Damascus Road experience? Did he not have an encounter with God that turned his life around?

Bear in mind the simple definition of children's spirituality—a child has ways of connecting with God, and God has ways of connecting with children. Insensitively delivered questions about eternal salvation are not understood (at best) and manipulatively detrimental (at worst).

There are a variety of views on the ways in which children come to faith. I strongly recommend the work of Ron Buckland,[7] although it can be hard to get hold of in print. He suggests seven possible responses to the question, "*What is the status of children before God?*" I would add that even within a single church, there is likely to be a range of beliefs amongst the individual members.

Here are seven possible responses that he addresses:

1. *All children start life outside the Kingdom of God.*

This assumes that children are sinful, and if they die before repentance and faith, they are destined for hell. It paints a somewhat hopeless situation for all those who are cognitively unable to process spiritual truths. A baby or a young child, for example, is clearly unable to understand the terms "repentance" and "faith" and make a response to them.

If this is a belief that is pertinent to your church, then there should be urgent evangelism amongst children, for surely the thoughts of children dying without God is almost unbearable to think of.

Augustine perpetuated the idea of "original sin" from his understanding of Romans 5:12.[8] This *actual* term is not found anywhere in the Bible (although Paul talks of the penalty of sin which marks us all); and it is worth noting the context in which Augustine used the term—he was addressing a perceived softening toward sin that bothered him greatly. Augustine saw baptism of infants as the way of salvation, which is Buckland's fourth possible view.

I want to be absolutely clear at the outset of this book that sin and rebellion amongst our children is a reality. Sin is part of our DNA, our gene pool. I once heard someone say, "No one needs to teach my child how to be naughty." And yet we must balance this with Jesus' words about children and the Kingdom of God. We must also bring into this equation thoughts about safeguarding (child protection), and the requirement to allow children to make their own choices from information presented to them. Scaring a child into the Kingdom is just not permissible and may end up backfiring on us later in life—at best with an angry and resentful teenager or at worst with an investigation into our activities by external agencies. We need not force the Good News; it has power all of its own to draw men, women, and children to God (see Rom. 1:16). I hope that our initial examination of children's spirituality will encourage you that developing a relationship with God is a natural journey for children. In Chapter 2 we will look further at this idea of "nurturing faith."

Proponents of this first view may struggle with these verses:

> *Then people brought little children to Jesus for Him to place His hands on them and pray for them. But the disciples rebuked them. Jesus said, "Let the little children come to Me, and do not hinder them, for the kingdom of heaven belongs to such as these." When He had placed His hands on them, He went on from there* (Matthew 19:13-15).

While the meaning of the words "kingdom of heaven" may cause some difficulties (is that the same as being "saved"?), it is clear that Jesus is saying something really important about children and the kingdom.

2. *The presence of a Christian parent establishes right standing before God.*

At its starkest, this view holds that the presence of at least one Christian parent gives the child right standing before God. This is based on teaching about the covenant, where the children of those under this special agreement belong to God, such as in the Old Testament with Abraham (see Gen. 17) and Israel (see Deut. 29).

So Christian parents have children who, at birth, belong to God because their parents have become His chosen people (see 1 Pet. 2:9-10). If this belief is strongly held by a church, one would expect to see evangelism amongst parents (or a desire to have many children), because then the people of God would grow exponentially!

3. *The presence of a Christian parent creates privilege, not standing.*

Buckland states that this third viewpoint "makes no claim about the child's status before God,"[9] except to say that the parent's influence is important. This is undoubtedly true, if our teaching *and* our life's example point to Jesus. This is supported by other research which will be covered in Chapter 2. Concentrating on the things which are most important for us as readers, be we church leaders or interested adults, I'll merely highlight his statement that the most influential primary setting for a developing human person is the family.[10] This privilege is also demonstrated in the writings of Horace Bushnell, who described the family as "the primary agent of grace" in a child's life.[11]

This is another reason to engage in evangelism and outreach to parents, who can then create a spiritually nurturing atmosphere in which to bring up their children. We'll have a deeper look at this point, and how we might facilitate this throughout this book.

4. *The experience of baptism establishes right standing before God.*

Children are brought by their parents in an act of dedication, to bring them up in the church and in the knowledge of God. The promises made are closely linked to the previous view. Some denominations want children to be baptized as soon as possible. This fourth view has led some denominations to clarify the wording in baptismal ceremonies.

5. *The experience of baptism enhances privileges.*

This is a softer view of number 4 above in that it expresses a belief in a future hope that the child will "in time" acknowledge Jesus as their personal Savior. The parents or godparents are key players at this event.

6. *All children belong to God.*

Every year I teach on this topic to a school of ministry. I always ask the students about the status of children before God, and nearly all of them choose this option as their preferred one. I then push the students to justify their response. It is usually very difficult for them to do so. They usually respond that this is an answer that "feels" good and right. If God is love, then how can children be hell bound? It means that all children enter Heaven irrespective of their status.

How do pastors feel about this one—that all children belong to God? Does this mean they are "saved" by merits of being children? Nearly every church I know engages in some form of evangelism or outreach to children. The work of Scripture Union and many other agencies reaches out to young children as well as teenagers, so clearly this sixth position cannot be held to be true, or therefore, there would be no need of evangelistic activity amongst children. If you hold this position, that children are received into Heaven by God simply because of the fact that they are children, how do you know when a child moves from the "saved" position to the "unsaved" position? Is there an age at which that happens? This is difficult ground, theologically and practically.

We need to look at a seventh possible option alongside what Jesus said about children.

7. All children begin with God, but will drift from that position unless an effective nurturing or evangelistic influence operates in their lives.

This seventh view bears repeating. According to Buckland:

> ...all children start with God but they will drift from that position unless an effective nurturing or evangelistic influence operates in their lives. It is a belongingness that may become rebellion.[12]

This possible view takes into account that children have a special place in God's heart; Jesus welcomed them and held them. We must not assume that children will reject His loving arms, and this is where children's spirituality, addressed at the beginning of this chapter, is an essential prerequisite to thinking about the status of children before God.

We can be certain because of the truth of Scripture that children are predisposed to sin, to making wrong choices; therefore, the starting point for pastors and leaders is to ensure that everyone in the congregation understands that nurturing a child's spirituality is a number one priority. This is not purely the realm of parents or the children's ministry team. Ignore this, and you miss a huge opportunity to grow your church in every sense of the word.

A child's turning away from Jesus will be "by degrees";[13] therefore, it is still essential to consider strategies which introduce children to a living relationship with the Lord Jesus. In other words, we still need to evangelize children—tell them the good news *and* provide ways for them to respond to that which is appropriate to their age and stage of cognitive development. We'll look at this further in Chapter 2. This is particularly important when children have suffered abuse and cruelty. It is possible for their natural spirituality, which draws them toward a loving God, to be dulled or damaged; and they are therefore unable to respond to God in the way that they might otherwise, had they been raised in a stable and loving home.

This seventh option of evangelism and nurture also helps those who feel slightly left out if they find it hard to put a specific date on when they became a Christian. They might say: *"I can't remember a time when I didn't love Jesus."* On the face of it, they don't have a dramatic testimony. Yet sometimes in our churches we celebrate the "wow" testimonies with claps and cheers, leaving those who have known faith in Jesus for decades or years feeling slightly second class. I have heard people say so many times, in an apologetic tone, "I don't have a dramatic testimony."

Yet how much there is to celebrate in the life of a child who loved Jesus, grew in love for Jesus, and walked with Jesus into their adult years!

JESUS WORDS' ABOUT CHILDREN

The encounter that takes place between Jesus and children is recorded in three of the Gospels:

> *People were bringing little children to Jesus for Him to place His hands on them, but the disciples rebuked them. When Jesus saw this, He was indignant. He said to them, "Let the little children come to Me, and do not hinder them, for the kingdom of God belongs to such as these. Truly I tell you, anyone who will not receive the kingdom of God like a little child will never enter it." And He took the children in His arms, placed His hands on them and blessed them* (Mark 10:13-16).

> *People were also bringing babies to Jesus for Him to place His hands on them. When the disciples saw this, they rebuked them. But Jesus called the children to Him and said, "Let the little children come to Me, and do not hinder them, for the kingdom of God belongs to such as these. Truly I tell you, anyone who will not receive the kingdom of God like a little child will never enter it"* (Luke 18:15-17).

> *Then people brought little children to Jesus for Him to place His hands on them and pray for them. But the disciples rebuked them. Jesus said, "Let the little children come to Me, and do not hinder them, for the kingdom of heaven belongs to such as these." When He had placed His hands on them, He went on from there* (Matthew 19:13-15).

Jesus was not talking in parables in the accounts in the verses above. He wasn't saying "become like a child" in an abstract way. So much has been read into this phrase; various Bible commentaries have translated this phrase as *"becoming receptive, amenable, simple, teachable, modest, unspoiled, trusting, in need of instruction and sinless."*[14] I don't agree with all of these words! In these verses, Jesus was physically taking real, human children, touching them, and elevating their status to all who were watching and listening.

He was not talking about adults with childlike qualities. Yes, we are to emulate some of what we see. Yes, we are to uphold the values that make children unique, for we can't physically regress back to childhood. But are we to see the Kingdom through the eyes of a child? Jesus was clarifying the relationship between children and the Kingdom. He said the Kingdom of God was theirs, literally *"belonging to such as these is the kingdom of God."*

Judith M. Gundry points out that the Greek language "uses a genitive of possession to describe the relation between the kingdom of God and little children such as those brought to Jesus: the kingdom is theirs. Thus it is appropriate that they now receive it."[15]

In the light of the Kingdom belonging to little children, Jesus was issuing a life-changing message, utterly counter-cultural. The commentator C.E.B. Cranfield notes:

> *The reason* [why the kingdom of God belongs to little children]...*is to be found in their objective humbleness, the fact that they are weak and helpless and unimportant, and in the fact that God has chosen the weak things of the world* (1 Corinthians 1:26ff).[16]

It is no coincidence that each of these Gospel accounts is followed by the story of the rich young ruler who was unable to let go of his possessions and intellectual reasoning. What a stark contrast! What point were the writers making by placing these stories side by side?

This brief scholarly exegesis of the Mark passage illustrates something vitally important for readers who teach or instruct others. Have we ever interpreted these words to refer only to adults who are like children? Don't these verses have potential to recalibrate how our faith community views children? Have we over-emphasized our role as the perceived fount of all knowledge instead of learning from a child's place in the Kingdom?

Children occupy a very special place in God's heart. I think He created it to be so. I suggest the rest of this book be read with this as our axiom:

All children begin with God, but will drift from that position unless an effective nurturing or evangelistic influence operates in their lives.

Chapter Two

EVANGELISM AND NURTURE

CULTIVATING SPIRITUALITY

We ended Chapter 1 with the challenging thought that Jesus' message about the Kingdom and little children was counter-cultural and profoundly challenging for people of that day. I would argue that it is the same for us today.

Jesus said the Kingdom of God was theirs, literally *"belonging to such as these is the kingdom of God,"* and Judith M. Gundry points out that the Greek language: "uses a genitive of possession to describe the relation between the kingdom of God and little children such as those brought to Jesus: *the kingdom is theirs*. Thus it is appropriate that they now receive it" (emphasis added).[17]

It is the very fact that children are weak and helpless and unimportant that they need help—intentional and targeted guidance and support. They grow up to face temptations, and struggle with desires to make wrong choices while battling with the challenges that arise from growing bodies and expanding minds. As Jesus said, a narrow path is before them (see Matt. 7:13-14).

Is it any wonder that there is a battle over our children's lives? If you and your church do not have plans for your children's spiritual growth and development, there is one who does—satan. Throughout history, he has come up with many strategies to remove children from the loving godly influence of adults.

Consider the following:

- Egypt's Pharaoh ordered that all Hebrew baby boys were to be drowned in the river Nile (see Exod. 1:22).

- Herod ordered the murder of baby boys following Jesus' birth (see Matt. 2:13).

- Exposure of infants occurred in the Roman Empire. The Twelve Tables (the earliest Roman code) gave fathers the right to practice infanticide.

- There was ancient and continues to be modern day termination of pregnancy.

- Abuse and neglect are rampant.

- The insipid "taking out" of children occurs as they are plugged into electronic equipment, to the point where portable consoles might even be brought to church services, so that their interaction and involvement in a faith community is reduced. In home meetings, DVDs and separate rooms may also further serve to "remove" children from the faith community.

I am aware that the last point seems controversial and perhaps a little judgmental, but please continue reading. It may not be your church experience, but I wonder if you might read on as this *does* happen in churches in this world. I am gravely concerned about "infotainment" provided by many children's programs, plus three-course snacks for any time spent worshipping in "adult church," just to get children through the time in gathered church. I have personally witnessed both. Surely there must be something more than this to help children remain part of the Church of Jesus? It's meant to be dynamic, life changing, influential, experiential, involving the littlest and the least, not something to be consumed or benignly tolerated until teenage-hood.

This need to be entertained, plugged in to a screen, or ignored seems to me to be another feature of Western Christianity that has satan rubbing his hands together with glee. Perhaps the overt taking out of children is not needed when our consumer mentality is doing quite well at disengagement without any further help.

The bulleted points presented above have one thought in common— they *deaden, damage,* and *dull.* They *deaden* spirituality, either by physical death, or by *damage* to the human spirit spirit, or by *dulling* the child's spirituality—their way of being with God and God's way of being with children.

If anything in this book's vision for the future is truly God-given, where a day is coming when significant numbers of children and their parents will seek and find Jesus, it will involve overt supernatural encounters occurring spontaneously and perhaps fuelled by a concerted missional movement arising from a praying and loving church that spans denominations and human divisions.

Imagine what it would look like if children, teenagers, and their parents with no faith background at all, who know nothing of the stories of Jesus, start to come along to your gatherings in significant numbers. As few as three or four families could change the dynamic of some smaller churches, and some fifty families would have a considerable impact.

It was with a mixture of excitement and incredulity that I read the following question from a working mother in a column in one of the UK's quality newspapers. She was seeking advice from the well-known TV presenter Mariella Frostrup:

> I feel angry a lot at the moment—I'm taking it out on my husband, and because my two-year-old is inseparable from him I'm worried I'm also hurting him when I head for the front door. I'm so frustrated. I'm the main breadwinner and I work 60 hours a week while my husband and mother-in-law look after our children. It's the best-case scenario, but it drives me mad. My husband constantly whines about how tired he is from his 27-hour working week. When I'm at home I'm in primary care of the children. I would find the sick feminist joke that is my life funny and enjoyable if I was appreciated, but I'm not remotely. I have my character assassinated on a daily basis. *Do you think church is the answer? I don't believe in God, but all that singing and being grateful has to help, surely?* (emphasis added).[18]

I read this woman's desperate questions just days before I finished an edit of this book, and I felt a deep urge to include this story in this chapter. This precious family is who we are to be ready for—will you love them with me? There were a variety of comments in the online section of the newspaper following Ms. Frostrup's reply, suggesting that the advice given back (*"Why not check out church?"*) was written sarcastically. I know that this working woman's scenario is probably true, as I personally have met women who have expressed the identical sentiment to me. *Something* is drawing them. Let's be ready to welcome whole families coming to check us out, coming to a church gathering so that they do something together and experience something different from consumer-led weekends.

I have been greatly impacted by watching DVD footage of the Church in China.[19] What has struck me is that all ages are involved in intense and intent worship and prayer, seeking God for their nation. Village and city worship services and outreach events appear to involve all ages together. An outdoor meeting shows children and adults presenting a drama before the Good News about Jesus is proclaimed, and then there is prayer for the blind, deaf, lame, and demonically oppressed. I am sure there are times when the age groups are separate. For example, there is footage of children being educated in Christian schools, but there is a clear expectation that these children will be the vehicles for their parents to be introduced to Christ.

Have we defaulted too much the other way? Have we separated the age groups most of the time for multiple reasons? In addition to these questions, we should also ask a few other questions regarding the current organization of our churches:

- What shape does your church currently have? A large gathering? A small group meeting in local communities? A combination of both?

- Where do children go when they enter the building? Do they stay with their parents? Are they taken to classrooms through a registration system? What acknowledgment is given to their presence in gathered worship? Does this matter?

- And what about teaching and discipling these new folks? Do you address just the parents in the hope that they'll pass it on to the young?

- Or do you have an intentional program of discipleship for the young as well?

- Where does this take place? In traditional Sunday school in a church building, or in homes?

- Who conducts this discipling? Parents? Paid staff? Children's ministry volunteers?

- Who trains them in how to do this effectively?

Think about this list of questions and about the kinds of challenging issues that will arise if a whole bunch of young people come with their families to your church or turn up on their own. My experience is that handling these issues needs to be *thought through in advance*, not left to chance. These young people are too precious to lose.

In the last chapter we looked at seven viewpoints on the status of children before God. I suggest that we use the seventh position as a helpful axiom for the remainder of this book:

All children begin with God, but will drift from that position unless an effective nurturing or evangelistic influence operates in their lives.

RESOURCES OF EVANGELISM AND NURTURE

I have made the assumption that readers are familiar with different models of bringing the Good News about Jesus to children and families. On my website,[20] I have appended some further information on this topic, should you wish to use it to help you audit what you currently do. It is by no means an exhaustive list.

Great background reading about the need for children to be reached with the Good News is contained in Occasional Paper 47[21] of the Lausanne Committee for World Evangelization, a worldwide movement that mobilizes evangelical leaders to collaborate for world evangelism. Children are the world's most unreached people group and are found *everywhere*.

There are also huge swathes of resources given over to help churches *evangelize* children—VBS curricula (USA), Scripture Union midweek and holiday club material (UK/further afield) are just two examples. But what material can we buy on the shelves to *nurture* children's faith?

Any resource that you use with children, that allows you as an adult to engage with children, is an opportunity to nurture growing faith. So, for example, it could be a Sunday school lesson, school lessons about the environment, or any opportunity to engage with children in simple conversation.

No entity is as ideally placed in society or in the world to nurture faith as is the Church. Before delving deeper into this, it's worth thinking about how faith grows. We are familiar with the idea of the Christian faith being something that develops over time with what we might call "good discipleship." But it also grows and develops as a person grows emotionally and cognitively. Learning isn't just about acquiring knowledge; it's also about the way responses are made as a result of certain stimuli around the learner. In other words, the environment around the learner is of extreme importance.

HEAD INFORMATION VERSUS SUPERNATURAL REVELATION

Ted Ward, professor emeritus in educational ministry and mission at Trinity Evangelical Divinity school, asks some important questions about the learning environment. They are relevant for us who long to see the growth not only in the numbers of young people in our churches but in our ability to teach and train them in the Christian faith. He asks:

> In what ways is Christian development dependent on a base of knowledge? In what ways does spiritual development differ from or go beyond other manifestations of the human development process? What roles can educators, parents, and other members of the Christian community play which will contribute to spiritual development?

He goes on to make a vital point:

> In much of Christian education, schooling imagery and cognitive motives tend to overwhelm the Bible's own emphasis on experience, acting upon truth, and the more celebrative, commemorative and emotional qualities of God's involvement with humankind—especially as revealed in the life, death and resurrection of Jesus Christ. The sad habit of "keeping school" in the Church seems to be sadly rooted in the assumption that schools have better answers to the questions of educational strategies and logistics.[22]

In other words, traditionally we have concentrated on imparting head knowledge in the manner of a teacher-pupil relationship in a classroom setting. This just isn't cutting it any more, as children continue to leave in large numbers, which will be fully detailed in Chapter 6. The phrase "the revolving door" with regard to the church has been used before—in for a season, then out again. It's time to keep the young people in the church! Many churches have reached a plateau of membership, and many are actually declining. It has been pointed out that this is not a problem confined to just the young. In writing this book, I aim to think of the children *and* their parents/extended family—it's time to draw everyone in.

It's also likely that our faulty discipleship process is to blame. "Teach head knowledge and wait till the child is older"—at least a teenager, if not a young adult—before they are allowed to serve others, minister in the gifts of the Spirit, and pray for people (to name only three examples).

This faulty process is based on the emphasis of information transfer (secular education) rather than the development of a deep relationship grounded in supernatural revelation to children and young people and the ability to practice that which we talk about within a loving faith community.

To address this, we need to look at how faith grows and develops.

John Westerhoff's Theory of Faith Development

John Westerhoff has a long career as a pastor to several churches, and by his own admission in the preface to his book,[23] his teaching and approach to ministry concentrated initially on forming adults. He has also worked in Christian academia for decades, combining this with his service as an Anglican priest. Throughout his life he has constantly "asked questions" and "tried new things." I mention his background as I think it helps to know that he does not write from a position far removed from the local church. He believes that throughout history, we have swung between concerns for conversion and concerns about nurture, almost as if the two were diametrically opposed. *My sincere belief is that we need both*, which is why Ron Buckland's seventh position makes such sense to me. Westerhoff says: "nurture and conversion are a unified whole."[24] Conversion—repentance—turning away from that which is wrong—must be taught about and experienced by children — and this will happen more than once!

The four types of faith outlined below are helpful when thinking *not just* about children, but about people of all ages who make up our congregations. Westerhoff describes faith as a verb—a way of behaving. He points out that these are generalizations and not meant to box children or adults into distinct categories. At each stage I will add in some personal observations.

Stage 1 begins with an *"experienced faith"*—children first learn about Christ not by what we say or teach theologically but by the experiences they have connected with those around them. They sense, explore, observe, and copy the stimuli around them, and experience through interaction.

This stage is where children form their impressions of God from their experiences of Christians and church. This means that I would like to do all I can to ensure that the child's experience of church is marked by love, trust, and care. The volunteers who look after him/her need to be taught about the importance of these early days. The crèche/nursery therefore becomes a hothouse environment for demonstrating the love and faithfulness of God. The physical space becomes very important—clean, warm, well resourced. The volunteers who want to help in this area (not hard-pressed parents!) serve the youngest members of the congregation. Loving grandparents, aunties, and uncles become the voice and touch of Jesus to the babes they cradle. The community can help faith to grow— belief that children possess spirituality which we expect will grow to personal faith in a loving God.

Stage 2 is an *"affiliative faith."* This flows naturally from Stage 1, assuming the needs of experienced faith have been met during childhood/early adolescence. *Belonging* is key; membership of an accepting community of faith is important. A clear sense of identity is formed. For example, this is *my* church; we sing *these songs* as we gather together. The children join in with the activities of the community, such as storytelling or singing, and share something of the awe and mystery that holds the community together. The child needs to be accepted and to feel the sense of togetherness that a significant and trusted leader brings.

So I, as a pastor/team leader, make sure that I am visible and consistent in my love for and time with the children and young people. I ask my volunteers to give a regular and sustained commitment to the children so that relationship is built up and a group identity is formed. Again, physical space is important—for young people to have a place that is "theirs." Story cushions, rhythm, and routine are all things that help—although with teenagers a degree of flexibility (exhibited by skilled leaders) within a routine is preferable.

Westerhoff points out that the Church must be constantly aware of its story and tell it often.[25] Therefore, Christmas and Easter, all age services and celebrations are of immense significance to growing faith, not just to the young but to adults as well. We celebrate our shared story.

Stage 3. Providing the needs of affiliative faith have been met, the child/young person/adult then enters a *"searching faith"* phase, where he or she will question, experiment, and look at other points of view and finally arrive at a faith that works because it makes sense to them, rather than because someone else has taught them to believe it. This is a necessary part of gaining identity and a strengthened ability to trust in God.

This is a time that children and young people's leaders need to tolerate—and dare I say welcome—questions and comments that express doubt or fear. Here, in my personal view, is one of the most important quotes from Westerhoff's seminal book, written in 1976 but with deep prophetic significance for church leaders today:

> It appears, regretfully, that many adults in the church have never had the benefit of an environment that encouraged searching faith. And so they are often frightened or disturbed by adolescents who are struggling to enlarge their affiliative faith to include searching faith. Some persons are forced out of the church during this state and, sadly, some never return; others remain in searching faith for the rest of their lives…we must remember that persons with searching faith still need to have all the needs of experienced and dependent faith met, even though they may appear to have cast them aside. And surely they need to be encouraged to remain within the faith community during their intellectual struggle, experimentation and first endeavours at commitment.[26]

Key here is the word *"community."* In the next chapter, we will explore a little more about the communities of the Bible that families with children belonged to. But we can say this at the outset: the community must be awash with the love of God that accepts the fragile newborn as much as the cute toddler as much as the difficult, moody teenager. I also firmly believe that many adults remain at this questioning stage and struggle to find acceptance in a community of faith.

Stage 4. Once the needs of searching faith have been met, *"owned faith"* should follow. This is a mature holding together of that which has been taught so far, alongside a demonstrated change in behavior and attitudes. The person with owned faith tries to show it by both word and deed. At this stage the Christian is prepared to make a stand for their faith in the face of opposition.

WHAT CAN WE LEARN FROM WESTERHOFF?

It's all very well to read about a theory, but what can we who lead churches or shape young people learn from these four stages?

1. Faith is growing and dynamic.

It is tempting to determine an age related to each of these stages, but that isn't always possible. I know young people who demonstrate all the hallmarks of owned faith and live for Jesus with a passion that is fiery and infectious. Yet many adults have not progressed in their faith past the first couple of stages, preferring the "warm fuzzy" stage of belonging and not yet appreciating the lifelong cost of following Jesus.

Note that in Westerhoff's categories, the conditions for one stage have to be met before advancement to the next. These conditions are vitally important for lifelong discipleship to occur—everything from the warmth and furnishing of the rooms, to the love and care shown by the adults to the very young plays a part. The "whole package" is needed. Lovely rooms on their own won't do it if the faith community manages to just tolerate children (knowing that a "good" church should have children in it); but neither will lots of loving adults working alongside children in cold and bare rooms give a consistent message. Think of the gardening metaphor—we want the optimum growing conditions for the seedlings to flourish.

And is it possible that the simple love and trust exhibited by children who love Jesus because they have been taught that He loves them, is, in God's eyes, *faith in Him?* Trust has been exhibited at the cognitive level of development appropriate to those young children.

Westerhoff uses the analogy of a tree to describe the growth of faith in developing human persons. He says: "a tree with one ring is as much a tree as a tree with four rings";[27] in other words, experienced faith is as valuable for a person to possess as owned faith.

However, he makes it clear that faith is a journey, and the goal should be to move toward owned faith, which is the point at which one would lay their life down for their faith. I want to make it clear that repentance, and saying sorry, for the things the child does wrong is a vital part of this journey, which leads neatly into further points to pick up from Westerhoff.

2. Children and young people need to make the faith and belief their own—just the same as adults!

The searching faith phase indicates that a period of questioning is natural and normal and may in fact be necessary for young people to fully commit to the Christian faith. It is therefore helpful for a child/teenager to have *experiences* of God as well as lots of information, head knowledge, about Him. This helps that young person weigh up whether he or she wants to know more about Him!

It is possibly at this stage that a lot of youngsters give up on the church, as they weigh up and test what they have been told. We as leaders must not be afraid of letting young people try things out, ask (what seems to be) antagonistic questions, and disagree with our theology. Patiently loving them through this time is a must if we are to retain our children.

I think it's really important not to walk in expectation of rebellion. There is a difference between asking questions because the young person sees a disconnect between what they are being told and what they see, and *outright* rejection and rebellion.

Because we suspect that the end result might be rebellion, we (parents/leaders) may tend to "crack down" on questions or attitudes on display that we feel we have already answered or should not see, and become impatient, intolerant, and perhaps even angry with the young person. Consider the following questions which seem entirely logical to me:

- *How do I know He is with me if I don't feel He is near?*

- *Am I just to believe without substance?*

- *How do I know God still does things today like the amazing things in the Bible?*

Is this rebellious talk? Or are these not genuine questions from a child or adolescent at the "searching phase" of faith development?

The role of the pastor/parents/adults involved with young people at this point of their faith development is one of loving acceptance, not rebuking. Instruction *is* needed, but only after we have exhibited:

a) patient listening to the young person's verbal expression as this allows them to draw their own conclusions;

b) good modelling of the truth of Jesus' words as lived out by us as adults; and

c) opportunities to experience (practice) the things read about in the pages of the New Testament.

*I am absolutely convinced that if these three actions are **determined and sustained practices** by the church community, the haemorrhage of children, teenagers, and young adults from the church will be arrested,* and we will end up with confident, secure adults who have "owned faith." The church community I grew up in exhibited these three practices in abundance.

Here is a concrete example. At the time of this writing, I have a pre-teen daughter exhibiting sophistication and maturity (in some ways) far beyond her genetic age. She has loved Jesus for as long as she can remember. She has been taught about repentance, about how sin separates us from God and how confessing the things we do wrong and our own selfish attitudes regularly keeps the relationship between us and God close. Yet, she has times where she doubts her beliefs. She has moments, regularly at the present time, where she will sit with me and say: *"What if I'm wrong, or you're wrong? What if Heaven doesn't exist? What if it is all a fairy tale?"*

My reaction could be one of deep disappointment, or even anger. Does she not know after all these years of being taught, that God is faithful and true? Is she rejecting the faith of our family outright? What if she says these things in her young people's group? Woe is me; I am a pastor after all!

But we listen patiently. As parents we reassure her of our love for her and tell her that it is entirely natural to have these thoughts. We let her express them in whatever way she wants to—sometimes this is with tears. We share with her that we also have doubts sometimes; and when she is ready to listen, we tell her stories of the perseverance of saints who have gone before us. We chew over some Bible passages with her, such as First Peter 1:6-9 and talk together (not lecture or teach) about what it means to have testing times, and what reward there is ahead for those who love Jesus even though they haven't seen Him. We tell her how Jesus poured out His heart for us in John 17:20ff and how He lives now to intercede for us.

In short, we offer instruction without loving her any less, nor worrying unduly, nor being either disappointed or angry; and we share honestly about our walk with Jesus and testify as often as we can in daily conversation about God's interaction in our lives. We love her through each and every episode of negative outpourings and deep questioning. I am confident she will continue to walk through this stage into owned faith—the mature holding together of all things. This demonstrates just how key the teenage years are for people to love youngsters deeply and listen wisely.

I have become even more convinced that a much more joined-up approach to children and young people is required.

3. An accepting and nurturing community is needed. Love like we might have never shown before.

It therefore follows that the church community must exhibit deep love toward children and young people. They are to be places where children *and* teenagers are valued, can make mistakes, can try things out, and most of all can be loved and accepted as individuals who are very special to God.

My observation is that young children, babies, and toddlers are easy to love. They are smiled at, passed around, and cooed at. We want to have them in our church as "signs of life." Children who tear around, fidget, and make noise during quiet moments of our services are not quite so easy for some of us to love, particularly if they pick their noses or emit smells. Pre-teens who question everything and might have rather a lot to say can be quite annoying. And insolent, sullen, undemonstrative teenagers are best left to their own devices at the back of the meeting room!

My point from this unflattering and hopefully (!) inaccurate pen portrait is that we can tend not to be consistent in our love toward the younger generations. Maybe we are getting only what we deserve when suddenly the younger generations appear to have left the church? Are they a chief consideration in the plans of your church? Ignore these stages of faith development and you risk losing a chunk of your church's future. Look for those with a heart to love on your children and young people, and encourage parents and the whole congregation to *love well*.

Paul writes:

> *Love is patient, love is kind. It does not envy, it does not boast, it is not proud. It does not dishonor others, it is not self-seeking, it is not easily angered, it keeps no record of wrongs. Love does not delight in evil but rejoices with the truth. It always protects, always trusts, always hopes, always perseveres* (1 Corinthians 13:4-7).

In the next chapter, we'll have a look at what the Bible says about family and consider the heartening news that no other institution on earth is as well placed as the faith community to see children and young people *fulfill their potential*—an oft-used phrase in education! It really means that we are a community who, under God's rule and reign, want nothing but the best for each other.

Chapter Three

FAMILIES IN THE OLD TESTAMENT

THE CONCEPT OF "TEAM"

In the last chapter, I made the assertion that there is no other organization quite like the faith community that serves as a place of nurture and spiritual growth for our young. In this chapter, I hope to reinvigorate parents and leaders with the idea that a reformation has begun. God is pulling generations together today to fulfill His divine purposes.

Consider this quote:

> Revival is not coming through the youth. It's coming through all ages connected. If you're alive and breathing God wants to use you for revival.[28]

In 2007, I led an all-age service on the theme of "all hands on deck." One of our prophetic artists, Ian, drew and painted throughout the service to produce *"The Good Ship QP"* (the church abbreviated its name to QP). In this painting, many crewmates were taking part in the sailing; some were climbing up the rigging, some were cleaning the decks, some were hoisting the anchor. Ian painted people at all stages of life: young, middle age, and those more senior. We were made to work together; not to work for our own gain, but to labor together on something not only bigger than ourselves, but bigger than our family, our church, our denomination.

I have never forgotten that painting as it has become a symbol of the future to me. And then, to read a quote which spoke to me in "the same language" on Twitter four years later still excites me and fires me up all over again. We were designed to be placed in families and be part of the family of God—the family of believers (see 1 Pet. 2:17). We are invited into community with the Father, Son, and Spirit, where we as children live under our Father's rule and reign, as part of His house. *In community with Him and with others.*

THE OLD TESTAMENT CONTEXT

In Ancient Near Eastern culture, you were who you were because of the family you were born into. So if your father owned land and farmed, so would you. If your father was a king, generally you would become one too. This is so different from the individualistic, free thinking that characterizes much of our thinking now. "You can be anything you want to be!" The American Dream, the idea that you can achieve anything if you set your mind to it, is an appealing prospect. Break the shackles of things that hold you back; walk away from abusive situations or extreme poverty; and with sheer grit, determination, hard work, and effort, you can rise above your circumstances.

This theory is praiseworthy in that it can instill hope and an ethos of hard work (so school teachers love it!). I used to teach Scottish fourteen year olds about what life might hold for American teenagers from three different ethnic groups—White, Hispanic, and African-American. A documentary series[29] showing their homes and schools had been commissioned, and it was fascinating to watch. Each of these young people discussed the American Dream and the belief that they could become rich and successful. For two of them, this belief had been spoken over their lives by parents, teachers, and other significant adults. But I still remember vividly the teenager who said she refused to believe in it. She said, "It's all broke," Because of the things she had seen—gang violence, abuse, and desperate poverty, she could not live under a false reality. She felt destined for very little, and she felt that way at just age fourteen.

In preparing this section of the book, I feel the Father is saying that we should not raise our young people to live under false hopes and expectations. Their life's worth should not come from having to dream up for themselves what *they think* might lie ahead for them. Children and young people need help to grasp how wide and deep the Father's love is for them and His purposes for them (see Eph. 3:17b-19). We, the faith community, have an incredible role to play in bringing Heaven to earth on this matter, as it is without doubt the Father's desire that our young ones understand the powerful reality of His love for them. We need to speak regularly and in as many settings as possible about the loving-kindness of Father God in order that they may be "filled to the measure of all the fullness of God." Lives surrendered to Him *will* result in fruitfulness.

"Come Back to the Father's House"

The principles I am going to share now are not meant to limit a person in any way, but in fact set them free *to be in the greatest place where destiny can be fulfilled—in their Father's house.* How prophetically significant is that phrase, when the Hebrew word is examined!

In the Old Testament, an individual was born into the nation of Israel, described by Gordon Wenham as "a giant firm or company in which every member had a specific place and a particular role to play."[30] He goes on to explain that every Israelite saw him/herself as a member of the firm and also members of a variety of teams. I think this has some significance for us today.

The first of these teams was the extended family, the next team was the clan, and the next again was the tribe. Successes and failures were shared amongst the team. So if the harvest failed, all the teams suffered. If sin was committed, it tainted the whole team and the firm.

Joshua 7:1 reflects this team concept when introducing Achan's sin:

> But the Israelites were unfaithful in regard to the devoted things; Achan son of Karmi, the son of Zimri, the son of Zerah, of the tribe of Judah, took some of them....

Verse 11 spells out clearly that this sin had caused a violation of the covenant between Israel and the Lord. All were affected by it, and it had to be dealt with, which is outlined in the remainder of Chapter 7.

In this story we see the structure of Israelite society. In verse 1 we read about "the son of..." (*the smallest unit, the nuclear family*), "the son of..." (*who were part of the extended family*), "the son of..." (*part of the clan*), of the *tribe* of Judah.

Verses 14-18 give fuller detail:

> In the morning, present yourselves tribe by tribe. The tribe the Lord chooses shall come forward clan by clan; the clan the Lord

chooses shall come forward family by family; and the family the Lord chooses shall come forward man by man....Early the next morning Joshua had Israel come forward by tribes, and Judah was chosen. The clans of Judah came forward, and the Zerahites were chosen. He had the clan of the Zerahites come forward by families, and Zimri was chosen. Joshua had his family come forward man by man, and Achan son of Karmi, the son of Zimri, the son of Zerah, of the tribe of Judah, was chosen.

So in this passage we see the societal structure:

Tribe (*shebet*)	Judah
Clan (*mishpachah*) – kinship group	Zerahites
Bet'ab (father's house) – family household	Zimri

Nuclear families lived in a house surrounded by two or three others, with a common courtyard in the center. This cluster of families, a husband and wife in one house, grandparents in another, a brother and his family in another, for example, was the extended family, the *bet'ab*—the father's house (in Hebrew).

Another example of this word in use is in Joshua 2:12-13, where Rahab speaks to the spies she has hidden in her house:

Now then, please swear to me by the Lord that you will show kindness to my family, because I have shown kindness to you. Give me a sure sign that you will spare the lives of my father and mother, my brothers and sisters, and all who belong to them—and that you will save us from death.

The extended family could number some fifty to one hundred persons as it consisted of male and female servants (and their families) and resident aliens, as well as the nuclear families. This is why Achan's family is described in terms of a father, grandfather, and great-grandfather—the extended families were part of the clan of Zerah.

So *bet'ab* could be the size of many small churches in the United Kingdom and many house churches or mid-sized communities in other contexts or countries. Keep this in mind when we get to Chapter 8!

THE WORDS OF OLD STILL SPEAK TODAY

What prophetic significance, if any, is there in all I have written so far?

Those who hold to a high view of Scripture would readily agree that the Old Testament has things to say to us today with regard to being the people of God. But how do we work this out in practice? On first glance, it looks as if our society is so different that very little can be gleaned for our circumstances. Moreover, theologians tell us to exercise care when reading the Old Testament with regard to our modern-day culture. However, having a historical and sociological awareness of generational structures, before reading the narrative passages about families and what happened to them for good and ill, can help us hugely today.

1. God's plan is for families to be blessed.

This is the non-negotiable starting point. I have seen this throughout my years as a children and family pastor. On an experiential level, it seems to me that God meets with gathered generations together in a very powerful way. If this is part of His plan for us, then we should not be surprised when it happens. I absolutely love watching it, in my own churches and in multi-denominational events I am leading. Tears often flow, greater love and respect toward one another is released, and a powerful sense of God's presence descends.

God's original design was for Adam and Eve to live under protection and blessing. The ideal for them was to raise children in the continual assurance of the Lord walking with them closely and providing for every need. The Book of Genesis spends a substantial amount of narrative describing God's heart for broken, torn-apart families—those of Jacob and Joseph.

In these two long accounts (chapters 25 to 35 and 37 to 50), there is incredible forgiveness and reconciliation between members of the family. And so blessing is passed on to the subsequent generations. This central premise of God's love has not changed; He created the generations and longs for them to walk in obedience to Him so that they would live under His blessing and protection.

2. God created the generations deliberately and for them to be blessed.

One of my thoughts for this book is to think a little broader about what we mean by "family." Yes, I have written and will write particularly about children. But children are part of something bigger; therefore, I have intended that what I write is for an audience of more than just children and their families. They are part of something that every human being is part of—a family, a generational line, one that stretches far back into the past and forward into the future.

God planned that we would have a society marked by different physiological generations, and in this regard, the Hebrew definition of *bet'ab* can be very helpful as it encompasses all generations together. He could have created human beings in any way He liked—monogenerational beings would not have been impossible for Him! And yet He chose that human beings grow, develop, and exhibit different mannerisms and abilities at different ages and stages of life, for we have a God who celebrates diversity and loves to create. Surely it gives Him great pleasure to see us as individuals and not swathes of characterless humanity. He specifically calls out to each and every generation:

> *Who has performed and done it? Calling the generations from the beginning?* "*I, the Lord, am the first; and with the last I am He* (Isaiah 41:4 NKJV).

Daphne Kirk helpfully gathers together some of the Scriptures that mention the word "generation."[31] The Hebrew word in each of these verses, *dor*,[32] refers to a period of time. Note the difference between human physiological, generational stages of life and "time periods."

- God's throne is from generation to generation (see Lam. 5:19).

- God's salvation and mercy are from generation to generation (see Isa. 51:8).

- God's dominion is from generation to generation (see Dan. 4:3).

- The plans of His heart are to all generations (see Ps. 33:11).

- His renown endures through all generations (see Ps. 102:12; Exod. 3:15).

- His faithfulness is from generation to generation (see Ps. 119:90).

We can therefore read these verses as saying "age to age," or in the case of the two Psalms references, for "periods of time without end" (like a circle). Every human person who has ever been or will be born is covered by the time period covered by God's rule and reign. *No one is left out*—not children, teenagers, young adults, the middle-aged, or senior adults. Generations today need to be healed, restored, and shown how it can be. There is a fractured aspect that has come into many so-called developed societies that sees each generation stick with their own for education, training, leisure, and spiritual development (for example: children's church, youth church, quiet traditional services for the older generation).

The Church of Jesus can model something that is different.

3. Sin has far-reaching consequences.

We see in the Old Testament how an entire "team" was marred by sin, because of the collective nature of society; the actions of one affected the whole. In our individualistic society, we tend to say that the opposite is the case—"My sin affects me and me only," but this is far too simplistic. I wonder if we do not have more connection to the Old Testament than we might think. In a family, one person's selfish actions, addictive behavior, and extreme temper can have a great effect on the whole family. The fragile spirit of a developing human person, a child, can be damaged by adverse family circumstances. Those who minister to generational bondages will substantiate to the hold the sins of the fathers can have on the present generation. Let's do all we can to encourage parents and grandparents to "cleanse the inside of the cup,"[33] as John and Paula Sandford describe in their classic book on restoring the Christian family. This means we do not discipline and instruct our children out of hypocritical hearts but out from a position of asking the Lord to work in us and cleanse us from our own selfish desires.

I see a lot of children who are marked by the effects of their parents' baggage. We owe it to our families to do all we can to live under the blessing and favor of the Father as, to be blunt, it makes family life easier!

So, parents, it is absolutely necessary to…

- forgive all who have wronged you and hurt you. Let go of your desire for revenge even if it feels as if the other party deserves it. In this way you prevent unforgiveness and bitterness building up which will not just affect you but will spill out on to those you have influence over.

- in particular, practice forgiveness unconditionally within your family, emulating the biblical pattern of Joseph and his brothers. Make room for God's great love and compassion to fill your heart as we see in David's love for Absalom (see 2 Sam. 13:39; 18:33).

- say "no" to things that are spiritually wrong, obtaining some outside help if needed.[34]

- love like there is no tomorrow. Use words and actions to bless your partner, children, church, and community.

- bring God's Word into your family life. This isn't just a matter of reading Bible verses, but talking about what God's Word is saying to you in each and every situation and its effect on your life and your children.

This is an application of the principle in the Old Testament that our sin affects the "team," the family, the clan, and the tribe. We see this in tendencies, habits, or addictions that can pass down generational lines as a consequence of sin.

Achan's story and Deuteronomy 5:9, which says that God will revisit the sins of the fathers upon the third and fourth generations, seem to be at odds with verses like Deuteronomy 24:16 and Ezekiel 18:19, which say that children are not to be put to death for their parent's sin, and vice versa. Achan's family must have been accomplices "in the know," in that they must have seen the devoted things or even help hide them. They knew from their own religious upbringing that stealing anything from God was utterly detestable to Him. They could not have been totally innocent, and we know from the New Testament case of Ananias and Sapphira (see Acts 5) that God hates subterfuge and deception.

The Ezekiel verse was written during the exile of Israel where, yet again, people were paying for the penalty of their sin. We read of this willful rebellion throughout First and Second Kings. There would have been young ones born in the exilic period who were therefore *not* personally responsible for what had happened; *they* hadn't broken their covenant with God Almighty. Yet they were tainted by the sin of their fathers and mothers. The overriding message of the prophet, however, is of the hope that is to come, that one day the nation would be restored. This foreshadows the coming of Jesus—that one day our atonement will have been achieved by the shed blood of an innocent Man who was also fully God.

4. The underlying ethos in the Old Testament was one of community and not individualism or consumerism.

In relation to point 2, despite what society may pressure us to believe, we do not live as isolated individuals. Our wrongdoing has an effect on other people. And in the goldfish bowl of family life—wrong choices, selfish actions, hearts and minds that live out of fear or insecurity or pressure to perform, unwittingly transfer their effect onto the young. This is why the extended family is described as the most significant team by Wenham.[35]

John and Paula Sandford ask, "What is a Christian family?" Their answer: *"It is simply a unit of warm human love where God raises His imperfect sons."*[36] Our churches are called to create communities of "warm human love." I think there is a growing "longing for belonging" today, perhaps seen in the question to Mariella Frostrup in Chapter 1.

5. Instruction, remembrances and celebration happened with all ages present.

> *These are the commands, decrees and laws the Lord your God directed me to teach you to observe in the land that you are crossing the Jordan to possess, so that you, your children and their children after them may fear the Lord your God as long as you live by keeping all His decrees and commands that I give you, and so that you may enjoy long life. Hear, Israel, and be careful to obey so that it may go well with you and that you may increase greatly in a land flowing with milk and honey, just as the Lord, the God of your ancestors, promised you. Hear, O Israel: The Lord our God, the Lord is one. Love the Lord your God with all your heart and with all your soul and with all your strength. These commandments that I give you today are to be on your hearts. Impress them on your children. Talk about them when you sit at home and when you walk along the road, when you lie down and when you get up. Tie them as symbols on your hands and bind them on your foreheads. Write them on the doorframes of your houses and on your gates* (Deuteronomy 6:1-9).

These verses form part of the *Shema*, a specific prayer whose recitation is commanded in the Torah. Instruction was a part of normal, everyday life, and verses like those above were given to the whole faith community, with an emphasis on threefold teaching—to the individual (*"commands I give you"*), to *"your"* children, and to the whole community (*"write them...on your gates"*). In verses 8 and 9, the verbs could conceivably cover every daily activity I partake in with my children—not a coincidence! The wearing of *tefillin* was a tangible physical symbol of verse 8.

These little leather pouches containing handwritten words from the Torah were bound tightly to the *arms* and the *foreheads*. These two places represent every kind of activity we do with our *physical bodies* or with our *mind and intellect*, and so remind us to keep God's *mitzvot*, His commandments in every setting we find ourselves. An interpretation of this symbolism for today's families who live in the light of the new covenant, where Jesus is the fulfillment of the Law, might consider using every opportunity to talk about God in very natural settings. For example, when chatting at home, when walking to school, in the car, or at bedtime prayers.

The people of Israel knew they were bound to a covenant with God, which had been given to Moses at Mount Sinai; and within the context of the home, they were to remind each and every generation of the Lord's faithfulness to them. In return, the Lord desired undivided loyalty and love from them. It is interesting to note the process whereby laws and instructions were given in an assembly, but the carrying out and enforcing of instruction happened in the *bet'ab*, clan, and tribal structures. Whatever way you examine—Israel individually, communally, familially— people were bound by love for God and bound to a desire to keep His commands and walk in the blessings of obedience.

Instruction also took place through the celebrating of festivals. Three are described in Deuteronomy 16—the Passover, the Festival of Weeks, and the Festival of the Tabernacle. Children were present at each one. It wasn't just nuclear families who joined together and remembered and celebrated; it was the whole community of faith bonded together in their love for the Lord and remembering His goodness and faithfulness.

The Old Testament outlines occasions where all the people were assembled together. Some examples include:

- Exodus 20—the Ten Commandments (and in Exodus 19, "all the people were summoned.")

- Deuteronomy 5—"all Israel was summoned."

- Deuteronomy 30—an address to the nation regarding prosperity if they turn to the Lord.

- Joshua 8—Joshua read to the whole assembly of Israel, including the women and children.

- Joshua 24—when the covenant was renewed, Joshua assembled "all the tribes."

Assemblies were an important part of Israelite life; and it could be an interesting as well as exciting exercise to consider where and when we assemble, all ages together, in our corporate life, to hear from God's Word. If we don't do this, it might be worth discussing why we don't. I am well aware that space constraints might prevent many congregations from doing this. Yet we should carefully consider if there is a way around this. Or is it simply not worth considering at all?

6. Children play a part on the "team."

They were not simply to be taught and instructed in a purposeless way, but to play *their* part in maintaining faithfulness to the covenant. I would suggest that this teaching and instruction is so that they join in with wholehearted submission and obedience to following the Lord's commands. They are members of the team.

There is a remarkable example of this in Second Chronicles 20:1-28. During King Jehoshaphat's reign, an enemy advanced toward the city causing fear amongst the people. A fast was proclaimed, and all the people of Judah came together to seek the Lord. King Jehoshaphat cried out to the Lord on behalf of the people:

> *All the men of Judah, with their wives and children and little ones, stood there before the Lord. Then the Spirit of the Lord came on Jahaziel son of Zechariah...as he stood in the assembly. He said: "Listen, King Jehoshaphat and all who live in Judah and Jerusalem! This is what the Lord says to you: 'Do not be afraid or discouraged because of this vast army. For the battle is not yours, but God's. Tomorrow march down against them. They will be climbing up by the Pass of Ziz, and you will find them at the end of the gorge in the Desert of Jeruel. You will not have to fight this battle. Take up your positions; stand firm and see the deliverance*

the Lord will give you, Judah and Jerusalem. Do not be afraid; do not be discouraged. Go out to face them tomorrow, and the Lord will be with you.'" Jehoshaphat bowed down with his face to the ground and all the people of Judah and Jerusalem fell down in worship before the Lord (2 Chronicles 20:13-18).

Children sought the Lord alongside the adults, and I think it's safe to assume they fell down in worship alongside the adults; this was a life and death situation. In the latter half of the story, they saw the Lord's great deliverance in winning the battle for their kingdom and for them. What a story they themselves would carry forward into adulthood and the raising of their own children. Surely this is the pattern we are to copy.

The power of instruction and training from parents and other members of the extended family and the clan is clearly seen in Second Kings 5, with the little Israelite servant girl. She has been forcibly removed from her own family and is now in a foreign land serving the wife of the powerful army commander, Naaman. He contracts the deadly disease, leprosy, and she is filled with pity for him:

She said to her mistress, "If only my master would see the prophet who is in Samaria! He would cure him of his leprosy" (2 Kings 5:3).

She knows about the prophet. She knows that God has power to heal. She knows that God can work miracles, because she would have seen them, sung of them, and been told of them. And through her knowledge, a miracle occurs. A mighty man takes steps of faith as a result of the actions and beliefs of a little girl. And is she not demonstrating the true missional potential of children to point the way to the One who heals and restores?

This story reveals a deep significance of the role of children and young people in the Bible. Without doubt, they challenge our stereotypes of children and what we think they are capable of. As we move into Part II of this book, we'll see how children can play a full part of the team, both within the local church and outside it, in taking the good news and their simple belief in a powerful God, out to their schools, friends, and families.

7. Which context do we minister in?

Understanding how instruction was given in the family setting in Ancient Near Eastern culture has a helpful resonance for us today. When we look in the next chapter, "Families in the New Testament," we will witness the continued importance of the extended household.

Ancient Israelite society contains the building blocks which foreshadow the Christian community in the New Testament—living for one another, looking outward to include the weak, vulnerable, and alien—working together as team. Therefore, we cannot afford to ignore what we hear about the family in this chapter.

Most of us will have great influence over a nuclear family, or over an extended family (*bet'ab*). Many of us can influence, teach, and train the clan or the kinship group. Still others of us can call out to the tribe. And all of us can teach that the primary place we belong is in the Father's house, the *bet'ab*.

At the end of Chapter 2, I suggested that there is no other institution or organization that can offer the nurturing and loving influence toward the young like the church community. Now, I would like to ask, does this assertion resonate with present-day studies of how children develop and grow?

FURTHER CONNECTIONS FOR TODAY

The field of psychology issues a stern warning against studying children in isolation without any reference to the environment around them. Len Vygotsky is a highly regarded developmental psychologist who has examined the connections between growing children and their culture (or community). Cynthia Neal outlines the Vygotskyian notion of children's development "being something that occurs in context (culture)" (i.e., they are heavily influenced by that which surrounds them), "and in turn *"transforms the context (culture)."*[37]

Although this study was written from a secular point of view, we might ask if children's ability to transform the context/culture transfers in any way to a faith development context?

It's worth taking a brief look at the work of Urie Bronfenbrenner who proposed that the growing human person is influenced by what he calls: *"a series of nesting structures, each inside the next, like a set of Russian dolls."*[38]

A child's immediate setting—the home, the classroom, the church—is called a microsystem.

The second level is called the mesosystem, which refers to the inter-connections between microsystems (for example, the connection between church and home). There are two additional levels—the exosystem and the macrosystem. However, at this time, let's address the immediate setting—the microsystem. It is proposed by secular developmental psychologists that children grow and develop in all their microsystems under the influence of *all the persons* within that microsystem.

Cynthia Neal states that the microsystems contain the building blocks of faith development,[39] and I agree. Ongoing, lifelong commitment to Christ is made or broken in them. Consider this alongside the information on the stages of faith development outlined in Chapter 2. Remember the need for a community that above all showed love and acceptance to the young person with questions. *Every single one of us in a church, whatever our attitudes and actions toward the young, is part of the microsystem.* How we react toward their presence has an influence upon them. Our willingness to include them, listen to them, and consider them in our church plans and strategy has an influence upon their growth and development.

Cynthia Neal also writes, "Children are to be part of a faith community and share in its life."[40] It seems as clear as day to me that this description from secular developmental psychology of "something that works" is describing Old Testament biblical practice. Yet again, experts describe something that we actually see was the original design of Creator God. His design for the development, nurture, and growth of young people is *the* best.

FURTHER IMPLICATIONS

As this book develops in later chapters, we have to seriously consider that leaving Christian education to a Sunday school setting only *removes faith from context and weakens the likelihood of lifelong discipleship*, as such separation of children from adults gives an artificial understanding of the Christian walk.

This is serious business, and we will look at how we can build strong practical foundations into church life to bring back together the big family of God.

Chapter Four

FAMILIES IN THE
NEW TESTAMENT

To interpret some of the words in the Bible about family and children, it is important that we understand that ancient languages did not have one word that is equivalent to the modern nuclear family. Rather, there were many words to describe households, family, and kinship ties.

In modern sociology, the study of *household* focuses on economics and functions. Studies on *family* tend to emphasis symbols, values, and meaning. A third perspective comes from the world of social anthropology, which I studied for a while as an undergraduate. This is the study of *kinship*, which sees family as part of a larger structure arising out of births and marriages. The whole area of genealogical study is now of increased interest to many in the United Kingdom, the United States, and elsewhere. People seem to be genuinely interested in where they have come from. I'd like to capitalize on this interest by addressing the factors that helped form the early Christian church in the New Testament.

RURAL AND URBAN SOCIETIES

We need to consider family in two settings. First, in the Gospels, the family context was a rural or small-town Palestinian setting. Further studies have shown that even here, the differences between wealthy families and peasants were increasing,[41] and stereotyping what every family looked like would soon not be possible.

So, what would be a good starting point? New Testament professor Halvor Moxnes provides some insight:

In the passage of Mark 10:29-31, we meet the family as a household; a group of people bound together by close kinship who live together and make a living together.[42]

The household was part of a larger social structure, the village. People participated in one another's lives. This harkens back to the last chapter when we considered the Old Testament people of God and is particularly seen in Luke and Acts.

The second setting of family is revealed through the New Testament letters which were written mainly in an urban, Hellenistic setting as the Gospel spread from Palestine throughout the Roman Empire to the Mediterranean cities. Society had developed (in sociological terms) into an *"advanced agrarian* (agricultural) *society."* This led to an accumulation of wealth rather than a subsistence way of life where each helped feed and look after the other. This increasing wealth and power gave rise to dominant individuals and families. The Roman Empire fanned this flame even further, with the ultimate power and authority resting with Caesar or his representatives.

So we see two geographical contexts—rural and urban, and two cultures—Judaism and Hellenism/Roman. Linguistically, there would be several languages as these two cultures mixed with even more at harbors and markets along Mediterranean trading routes. Economically, the differences between households increased. Moreover, Ancient Near East and Mediterranean culture was on the cusp of even more changes.

THE STRENGTH OF EARLY CHRISTIANITY

In view of these circumstances, Rodney Stark asks a profound question:

> How did a tiny and obscure messianic movement from the edge of the Roman Empire dislodge classical paganism and become the dominant faith of Western civilisation?[43]

Christianity flourished alongside one of the most widely recognized powerful forces in history—the might of the Roman Empire. Stark outlines a very conservative estimate of 40-percent growth per decade in the numbers of Christians, and admits that he comes to this figure without allowing any space for signs, wonders, and the miraculous;[44] therefore, he calls this a conservative estimate. He calculates that there would have been 1000 Christians in AD 40, rising to 33,882,000 by AD 350, more than half of the Roman Empire's population at that time (estimated at sixty million).[45] There seems to have been a remarkable increase in figures between 250 and 300, and this is borne out in archaeological evidence of houses being remodelled to accommodate more worshippers.

It's interesting to note that during this period, persecution increased under several Roman Emperors, most notably Valerian in 253. However, by 311, this lessened, culminating in Constantine's edict of toleration in 313. As an aside, there may be another lesson here: as persecution increased, the Church grew rapidly. Consequently, the governmental leaders realized that they needed the Christians on their side. (For example, in 311, Galerius realized he needed the Christians to pray for the security of the state.)

The fact that Christianity spread to the edges of the Roman Empire and beyond during the first few centuries after Christ's death and resurrection means that *vast numbers of people became Christians*, even though we cannot count them accurately. We must also remember that in the first two centuries, there was a *personal cost to conversion*. A Christian no longer swore allegiance to the Emperor, but to God. Christians were misunderstood and talked about with suspicion and even revulsion at times. Punishments for conversion varied from fines, to exile, to death; and any study of early church history will reveal numerous stories of Christians being martyred in tortuous ways.

This is an important context for true societal transformation.

THE TIES THAT BIND

Please note that in this section I am not aiming to simply reproduce historical facts, which are more fully explained in other publications, but I am asking you to keep this question at the forefront of your mind: *what relevance might the descriptions of what was happening have for us today?* Think about what the pagan observers witnessed.

Historians and sociologists have written extensively on the rise of numbers professing a conversion to Christianity. I will explore some of the reasons for this growth, although there are many possible reasons! Before I do so, let's think about what makes people more likely to convert to another faith.

Numerous sociological studies have noted that converts are usually united by close ties of friendship or kinship—next-door neighbors, mothers of similar ages, friends from work. The attachments are usually *direct* and *intimate*; that is, you share something of your life with the other person. This is why the first followers of any religion usually come from family and close friends.[46] This has been confirmed for Christianity, Islam, Mormonism, and the Moonies.

And so here lies a key principle in reaching families: *for conversion to happen, people have or develop stronger attachments to Christians than they have to non-members of Christianity.* We will consider the concept of looking out for "persons of peace" in a later chapter—these are people who "receive" you and are especially open to you. People who are not yet believers but who develop strong friendships with Christians are more likely to become Christians themselves. Therefore, it is important to ensure we make time for these friendships.

WOMEN FIND A TRUE "NEW LIFE"

In the first century, patriarchal ideology was the norm in both Roman and Rabbinic Judaism society. Women were seen as vastly inferior in both peasant culture and in the wealthy elite of the ruling Roman classes. Jesus challenged both patriarchy and social taboos. Nicky Gumbel gives the examples of Jesus speaking to a Samaritan woman in public, travelling with women disciples, and choosing women amongst His closest friends. He further states that "women were the last people to leave the scene of the crucifixion, the first to arrive at the empty tomb and the first witnesses of the resurrection."[47] These are major incidents and would have been noted by the early Christians. I suspect at least some women turned to this new faith because of the true new life it offered them.

In addition, at this time there was a low birth rate in the Roman Empire due to abortion and infanticide. Roman men frequently fathered children by multiple women while ordering their own partner to abort a pregnancy or dispose of a newborn infant. The population was declining,[48] which caused successive emperors some concern. To remain a power to be reckoned with in the ancient world meant having a population that exceeded the natural replacement level. Therefore, eventually, men and women were encouraged to have children—a minimum of three, but more were welcomed. The decline became so acute that at one point in the second century, Marcus Aurelius had to draft in slaves to fill spaces in the army.[49]

On the other hand, Christian women enjoyed higher rates of fertility and greater security, which is unpacked in chapter 5 of Rodney Stark's book and well worth a read when considering this chapter.

Because Christianity directly improved the quality of life for wives and mothers, is it any wonder that women turned to Christianity in vast numbers? Christian teaching directly confronted such horrors as incest, infanticide, abortion, infidelity, polygamy, and divorce. The Bible taught of a better way to live where each one thought more highly of the other than him/herself. Sexual purity and marriage were honored, and each life was valued. We cannot underestimate the sociological change Christian morality and ethics brought about. There was an increase in Gentile women's status, standing, and security. (Jewish women already enjoyed more honor and protection due to Rabbinic adherence to the Law.) Christian women possessed far greater marital security and equality than pagan women. Husbands were instructed to love their wives with the same love that Christ had for the Church—with tenderness and unfailing faithfulness. This was bound to have an effect on family life and draw even more people to the church.

The Low Status of Gentile Children

In the first-century Roman Empire, the man held power over everyone's possessions in the whole household—he was the *paterfamilias*. We have already briefly discussed the low birth rate in the Roman Empire during the time of the first Christians, but a closer look at the man's role in this will help us to understand even more the attraction of the Christian family unit.

As previously mentioned, there was a low birth rate. Infanticide was readily practiced, permissible by law, and advocated by philosophers. Under Roman law, fathers had the right to speak life or death over every newborn child, and male children were favored. In one archaeological excavation, the bones of over 100 day-old babies were found in the sewers under a bath-house.[50] In this case, it was not possible to ascertain if the children were male or female, but it is readily accepted that there were far more men than women in the population as a whole, due to the practice of killing newborn females.

Abortion was common in the Greco-Roman world as a form of contraception and was carried out by ingesting poison or by using surgically invasive ways with associated high risks, which ended the lives of many mothers as well as their babies. In the majority of cases, it was the men who made the decision to abort.

Children had a very low status in society. There are occasional glimpses in ancient literature of tenderness shown to children, but more commonly they were subject to brutal discipline. Their instruction was compared to breaking in or taming a wild animal. Plato said:

> Of all wild creatures, the child is the most intractable; for insofar as it, above all others, possesses a fount of reason that is as yet uncurbed, it is a treacherous, sly and most insolent creature. Wherefore the child must be strapped up, as it were, with many bridles.[51]

This wasn't just poetic talk. Children's nurses swathed them tightly so that their limbs could not move for long periods of time. Beatings were commonplace as force was seen as the only way to train children.

While initially, Roman fathers did spend more time with their sons instructing them in the home, the Greek model of education came to be adopted throughout the Empire, causing sons to be separated from their fathers to attend schools with their *paedagogus* (male childminder—often a Greek slave who accompanied boys to school to oversee their instruction). Stoic philosophers in the Greek world, writing about children between the ages of birth and seven years old, said they lacked reason and logic because of their inability to speak. It was this perception that led to the legitimacy of physical punishment as soon as child started weaning (at around 18 months old). This information explains why childhood was seen as something to be grown out of on the journey to puberty, which signalled the progression to adulthood and full legal status.

THE STATUS OF JEWISH CHILDREN

Jews differed radically from the Gentiles. The Law of Moses forbade infanticide and abortion, and contemporary Jewish writers like Philo of Alexandria reinforced this law. Marriage was important as a means of preserving the race and the best framework for child-rearing. In Jewish culture, children were seen as a blessing from the Lord, and having them was an act of obedience. Having numerous offspring ensured the continuation of the pure covenant people of God, the "holy race" (see Ezra 9:2).

Boys were educated in a knowledge and understanding of the Torah, not just by rote and repetition, but also *as it applied to daily living*. At first this was the role of fathers, but as with the Gentiles, schools became the preferred method of instruction, taking the form of synagogue-based schooling. And so we read of Paul's educational history in Acts 22:3, studying at the school of Gamaliel.

Girls were not taught reading and writing; in fact, this was seen as an utter waste of time, as their activities were to be restricted to the confines of the home. Girls were not seen as capable of learning, an important point to think about as we move toward some present-day reflections. Philo commented: "The attitude of a man is formed by reason, of woman by sensuality."[52]

It's important to note that differences in child-rearing became apparent as Jews moved to cities. Some families became less dependent on agriculture for their living and were influenced by the pluralistic cultures that existed in ports and trading posts in the Roman world. Whereas Palestinian Jewish parents working the land continued to highly value children for their ability to work alongside them, and provide emotional and social care as they grew older. In the centuries after Jesus' resurrection, we cannot strictly box Jewish culture "over here" entirely from Gentile culture "over there." The melting pot of Greek thought influencing Roman culture, plus other cults and sects who were influencing the population, meant that a wide spectrum of practices were evolving. It was this precise context that much of the New Testament addresses.

As with Roman children, Jewish children also had no status and were not regarded as a full person until they reached puberty. W.A. Strange describes children as *"true marginal figures in the society of the ancient world."*[53]

Jesus Elevates Families to Advance the Kingdom

This brief summary of the culture in which the Church was born shows how radical a change Christian beliefs brought to marriage and family life. Jesus condemned lust and adultery and elevated women and children by His attitudes and actions toward them.

Jesus valued children highly. He touched them, blessed them, and lifted them up as examples of faith and humanity. His words and actions in the Gospels were the necessary platform for the move of God throughout households in Acts.

It has struck me that perhaps Jesus elevated the status of both women and children in order that new building blocks be formed (i.e. households) for the advancement of the Kingdom. It seems to me that His words and actions to address inequalities and unrighteous behavior were especially to allow the bloom and development (and safety!) of women and children as persons made *imago dei.*

He *did* call into being a new community that called into question the absolute demands of the family and kinship group (see Matt. 10:37; Luke 14:26); but this was because He was calling people back to the place of a covenant relationship with His Father, the One who truly was the Head of His people, the Church. He was not anti-family but rather pro-Kingdom. Allegiance to God was the highest priority any family member should have. Individuals were also to challenge their families to put the Kingdom first.

HOUSEHOLDS AS PART OF THE CHURCH

I have suggested that societal transformation as a direct result of Jesus' teaching and the reorientation of lives allowed new building blocks to be formed.

Households became the main gathering place for the urban church. There were no church buildings; rather, believers met in homes in their household units. These were the natural networks of the day.

We mentioned earlier that although there is no single term for *family* in the New Testament, there are several other words that relate to the concept of family. One of these is *oikos,* meaning *house (of)* or *household,* and this included the householder's family, slaves, and even friends and neighbors. I would say that the people in my *regular* sphere of influence are my *oikos.* Each member of a family has unparalleled opportunities to attract other people into the faith, which you hold dear through each of your networks, because at the heart of *oikos* are natural relationships, which can form regardless of social class and background.

As individuals in each household entered into a personal relationship with God through Jesus Christ, changes occurred in their behavior, attitudes, and way of living that demonstrated this radical reorientation and clearly attracted others within their networks to join. Remember this was no peer pressure decision; this came at a cost, given the new allegiance that converts were forming to the one true God and not to Caesar and his gods.

Joel Green states that "community-nested practices"[54] came into individual families' lives that openly showed this new allegiance and opened the way for further transformation in family life, community, and society.

Extended households were the major pre-existing network in Rome, and when Christianity arrived and grew using the same pattern, exponential growth happened. There are many references to *oikos* in Scripture. I strongly commend Mike Breen and Alex Absalom's *Launching Missional Communities: A Field Guide* for comprehensive evidence on this subject.[55] I will cite their unpacking of Romans 16 which is directed to multiple households—*oikos* communities:

> This includes the household (oikos) of Priscilla and Aquila (v4-5) the household of Aristobulus (v10) (literally, it reads "the ones of [belonging to] Aristobulus", which is clearly an oikos concept), and the household of Narcissus (v11). Verse 14 says "Greet Asyncritus, Phlegon, Hermes, Patrobas, Hermas and the brothers with them". This references a distinct community, with the term 'brothers' (adelphous) simply a different way of saying ekklesia or oikos. This is then followed directly by verse 15, "Greet Philogus, Julia, Nereus and his sister, and Olympas and all the saints with them", which again implies another oikos community.[56]

A leading New Testament scholar James Dunn actually uses the term "Missional Communities" to describe these groupings in Rome.[57] At the start of this section I noted that *oikos* can mean "the house of" or the "household of." This Romans passage is the former, and the Philippian jailer and his family in Acts 16 are an example of the latter. I would suggest that the former can influence the latter; that is, the church meeting *at the house of X*, can have an impact on the community around it that brings *the household of Y* to a knowledge of God.

Oikos was almost certainly an open community. It did not mean that every member of a host-household was a fellow believer. In Philemon 10, we read that Onesimus was not a "brother" to Philemon until he had met Paul. Undoubtedly, unbelieving husbands and wives converted to Christianity through the witness of the growing church. Further numerical growth occurred from amongst the young. The regard for children radically changed from the prevailing practice in Greco-Roman culture of taming or breaking children as if they were wild animals.

Therefore, I believe the early church was operating under the principles I described in Chapters 1 and 2—*they were nurturing faith within their oikos communities.* It is worth reflecting how counter-cultural this was for the Gentiles who did not have the background teaching of the Torah or knowledge of the Deuteronomy 6 passage. Would this not be similarly counter-cultural for families who are new to the Christian faith today? Children connected with the one true God about whom they were taught—not just verbally but in modelling community and signs and wonders. They continued on in faith and lifelong commitment to Jesus (owned faith). I think this is proved in the testimonies from the ancients in the faith, such as Polycarp, who said he had been Christ's servant for 86 years.[58] Justin Martyr could point to "many men and women of sixty and seventy years of age, who became disciples of Christ from their childhood."[59]

CHILDREN AND FAMILY IN THE BOOK OF ACTS

I have often heard people ask why there is so little written about children in the Book of Acts when there is so much about children in the Gospels. Acts chapter 2 sees the power of the Holy Spirit poured out upon extended family networks which propels the Church outward even more. I am convinced that less was said about children because more was demonstrated about *community* (which children were part of) in the setting of the home.

Nevertheless, there are still some important examples of children being mentioned in the Book of Acts. Children were part of the life of the community as they were present in gatherings described in this Book. Eutychus, characterized as "a young man" and "a boy" in Acts 20:9,12, was raised to life after falling out of a window during a very long meeting. In Acts 21:5, men, women, and children knelt together on the beach and prayed publicly. The *oikos* communities did not just permit children to join in with worshipful activities; it became a natural extension of their lives together.

Very soon after the day of Pentecost, there is evidence that God wanted to presence Himself in *oikos* gatherings. In Acts 10:33, in Cornelius' home, all gathered *in the presence of God*. This is a very significant verse, as "house" and "presence" always referred to the temple in Jerusalem up until this point. So here we see a move away from a physical building with its associated religious practice function to gathering in homes with all ages present. It takes the worship of God once and for all out of the hands of priests and puts it into the reach of every believer.

Professor Joel Green contributes some important reflections on the Book of Acts which help us to consider what we might seek to build today. Green claims that implied all through the Book of Acts is the need for family transformation in order to impact the city. Households were actually very important to the Roman state. It was where order (admittedly, hierarchical and patriarchal) was found. It was the place where one began to walk out one's path in life. Hence, Cicero's famous phrase: "the household is the seedbed of the state."[60] Green points out that Rome regarded itself as a household with the emperor as paterfamilias—"in other words the centre of the Roman world was, first, the home...."[61]

This is incredibly significant in our thoughts for today. *As is His habit of doing so, God has redeemed something broken and sinful (the oikos household), to use it for His sovereign purposes—the redemption of the whole world.* Keep remembering that *oikos* is your own family, but *not just* your family—it's your extended household, your networks. God wants to restore relationships *with* every person who is a member of it and *between* every person in it and through it to reach other people with the Good News.

Within it, children are of the utmost importance.

Paul's Teaching on Children and Family

Paul clearly taught in First Corinthians 7:14 that children are *in* the community of faith, not out of it, and he specifically wrote about children in households where one partner is not a Christian. Although this verse is fraught with difficulties in translation and interpretation, for the purposes of this book it echoes true with my conclusions in Chapter 1 and 2—that the child of a Christian parent is in a position of privilege to be given numerous opportunities to grow and develop his or her own faith in Jesus because of the input from parent(s) and other significant adults in the extended community.

We do witness some apparent conflicts in how children are seen in the Epistles. D. L. Stamps describes it as thus:

> In the Epistles there is the general perspective that a child represents a state of development that one is to grow out of (i.e. immaturity) or a state of being that is unrealised potential (1 Cor 13:11, 14:20; James 1:6; Heb 5:13; 1 Peter 2:2). In the Gospels children represent an identity to which disciples should aspire and from which disciples learn (Matt 18:1-5, Mark 9:33-37, 10:13-16).[62]

Paul was writing to the fledgling Church to urge them to grow toward maturity. He wrote using a metaphor of the day—of the culture, with which his listeners and readers could identify. Don't hang around at the stage of childhood—head for maturity. So Paul was using a feature of the culture (that was to be subjected to change because of Jesus) to make a teaching point. Paul also used this feature in Galatians 3:24 to explain how the Law was like a *paedagogus* (guardian/tutor) to bring us to Christ, but now that we are His, the *paedagogus* is no longer required.

Whereas Jesus in the Gospels challenged convention, taboo, and stereotype with the values of the Kingdom, Paul used situations commonly understood within the culture of the time to encourage the believers to go on to maturity. Outside of Paul's writing, Peter wrote very positively (see 1 Pet. 2:2) urging the Christian to be like a baby with an insatiable appetite for the kind of food that builds him or her up to be a strong individual. So the state of childhood was not necessarily seen negatively.

There are some important points to note in Colossians 3:14 and Ephesians 6, in the "instructions for holy living," which were to be read out loud to the believers. These verses indicate that children were not only present in worship but also worthy of being given specific instruction. This was not just for them but also for fathers regarding their conduct with their children (see Eph. 6:4). The responsibilities are mutual. Strange puts it like this:

If children owe their parents the duty of respect, no less do parents owe their children the duty of consideration. This was quite a radical idea in the culture of time, where a far more one-way relationship would be the norm...Ephesians (builds)...a wider vision of a family which can be a living expression of life in Christ.[63]

It has often been suggested that Paul was not particularly pro-children. I disagree. *I think Paul was pro-discipling,* urging the Church of Jesus to become more like Jesus, which included *everyone.* These verses are a practical expression of Jesus' vision for the family, surrendered to one another, living to demonstrate something of the Kingdom of God. They are addressed to men and women, young and old, slave or free, Jew or Gentile – the family of God. Mutual submission rather than authoritarianism allows all members of the family to grow in their faith together.

THE FAMILY HAS BEEN REDEEMED

In the New Testament, the early church shared life together in natural networks of *oikos* relationships that grew and spread geographically across the Roman Empire. We have proof of this from archaeology (houses with enlarged meeting rooms), from Scripture (such as the Romans 16 passage), and from sociological research on Greco-Roman and Palestinian society.

I have four specific conclusions to make from this brief study of children and family in the New Testament.

1. *During the first two centuries of the church's growth, the family—that is, the nuclear family and the extended household—underwent a dramatic transformation. This in itself was a catalyst for conversion to occur.* I suggest that this drew all sorts of people to investigate what was happening amongst the Christians, and not just those who were yearning for a safe and secure environment in which to live and breathe themselves and to bring up children. Family life was turned around. *There was a dramatic change in the standing and security of women, the respect accorded to marriage, and the treatment of children.* We cannot underestimate how counter-cultural that was. For Jewish believers, there was a hearkening back to *bet'ab*—the father's house—where the extended family was found. For the Gentile converts, Christian *oikos* redeemed the family for God's purposes.

2. The Book of Acts rejects a separatist model of children and adults. The coming of the Spirit and the subsequent growth and spread of the church from town to province to country to continent occurred in these early centuries with all generations witnessing to new life in Jesus in community together. We will unpack this as we transition through Chapter 5 and on to subsequent chapters.

3. Children were a natural part of the church's corporate life and missional activity. This is revealed in specific Scriptures (for example, I have highlighted Acts 20, Acts 21, Colossians 3, Ephesians 6), and also in primary sources, such as Pliny who clearly noticed that children were part of the Christian worship practices that he abhorred. He said in 112 that *"many of all ages were in danger of contagion from the Christian menace."*[64] I think this is a clear indication that children (*"many of all ages"*) were open to missional influence—not just from adults, but I believe that children were missionaries themselves, playing, talking, and demonstrating what they believed to the children around them.

Remember the term *microsystems* in Chapter 3. Secular developmental psychologists cite that children grow and develop under the influence of *all the persons* within that microsystem—*oikos.* So adults with a heart for mission help produce children with this same heart. There is no subdivision of missional adults doing the "telling others" without their children being part and parcel of this lifestyle.

I have observed today a growth in encouraging children to be fully used by God as missionaries to their friends and schools, but it concerns me when it is entirely separate from the activities of their parents or other adults. *Oikos* gives security, safety, covering, and a solid ground. So in the early church there existed missional families living an incarnational lifestyle, which means simply that their lives were less about inviting people to events and more about modelling a way of life that stood out as different, in the ways I outlined throughout this chapter—that was deeply counter-cultural and undeniably attractive to others.

4. We should look for ways to reinforce and affirm existing oikos communities in our local churches today and make space to build new ones arising out of our networks. This means we need to stop being so busy and release each other to be "fully present" in our networks of friends, families, and neighbors, instead of always attempting to squeeze as much as we can into our days.

These four conclusions echo what Joel Green says about the Book of Acts. It forces us to reflect on the need to model community as all ages together; otherwise, we are left with something deeply concerning:

> Generations of children who are provided with less and less contact with faithful agents of Christian mission, fewer and fewer models of relationship-building, and so for whom faith becomes so personalized that it need not even find expression within one's own family.[65]

In the next chapter we will examine some attitudes toward children and adults in the church that may have prevented us from moving forward toward the model of inclusivity, which Professor Green clearly hints at in the quote above. The Church of Jesus Christ is the one institution on earth that can provide significance for every human being.

THE TURNING POINT

Chapter Five

STARTING AFRESH

Although I was convinced of the coming harvest of children and families into the Church of Jesus, I looked around at the numbers of children in the churches in the United Kingdom, and it was undeniable that we have been living in a state of marked decline in terms of the numbers of children attending church (see Chapter 6 for more details).

These circumstances continued to bother me, so I sat still one day in September 2008 to "enquire of the Lord," following David's example and his many times when he "enquired of the Lord" to seek strategy (see 1 Sam. 23:4, 30:8'; 2 Sam. 2:1, 5:19,23). I felt like I had nothing to lose by asking and seeing if God would say anything to me—the "nothing ventured, nothing gained" tactic! Specifically, I wanted to know what was preventing children and their families from coming into the family of God, from attending or joining our churches, in the kinds of numbers I wanted to see and that I believed I would one day see.

The following Scripture came to mind:

> *I will stand at my watch and station myself on the ramparts; I will look to see what He will say to me, and what answer I am to give to this complaint. Then the Lord replied: "Write down the revelation and make it plain on tablets so that a herald may run with it. For the revelation awaits an appointed time; it speaks of the end and will not prove false. Though it linger, wait for it; it will certainly come and will not delay"* (Habbakuk 2:1-3).

Using the passage above as a model, I asked the Lord to speak to me, to give me revelation and insight. In the Introduction of this book, I mentioned that I believe it is time for us to "make ready," to prepare the ditches for what is to come. I believe that God showed me 16 beliefs or actions that require attention and change if the Western Church is to see children and families find Jesus and become disciples in great numbers. In the context of this book, I present them humbly before you, the reader. I make no claim that any or all of these are true for your church. I simply ask that you weigh these things in your own thoughts and prayers, and simply ask God, Is there anything here that has marked the way I or my church has dealt with children?

If there is, what should be done about it? The simple answer is to repent—disassociate yourself and your faith community from these beliefs or actions. Say you're sorry, ask others to join you, and resolve not to go back to that way of thinking. Speak instead the truth, from your own knowledge of the children and families in your church, or from Jesus' own words about children.

This change in your heart and mind will allow you to get the most from the subsequent chapters of this book. You will be able to progress forward, knowing that you have let go of unhelpful attitudes, and the sin(s) that so easily entangle and snare you.

There is no condemnation in identifying with any of the sixteen points; we live in a world that is full of unhelpful attitudes toward children, and we have been tainted with these. We're not super-human! As you read on, decide that today is a time to break free of the world's ways of seeing young ones and to come afresh to Father God so that He can reenergize you with His heart toward children.

> *Therefore, since we have a great high priest who has ascended into heaven, Jesus the Son of God, let us hold firmly to the faith we profess. For we do not have a high priest who is unable to empathize with our weaknesses, but we have One who has been tempted in every way, just as we are—yet He did not sin. Let us then approach the throne of grace with confidence, so that we may receive mercy and find grace to help us in our time of need* (Hebrews 4:14-16).

1. We repent of simply tolerating children, and now see them as made in the image of God.

Explanation/Clarification

This refers to an attitude that may, on the face of it, accept children into the church community, but perhaps rather grudgingly, realizing that we "need" to have young people in our church for its future propagation. But perhaps, deep inside, there is a "toleration" of children rather than welcoming children with joy and gratitude. Taking into account that every human being is made *imago dei*—in the image of God, we are to celebrate every human person's presence amongst us as each one has inherent value that is not related to his or her current age, background, or standing in the community. This incorrect attitude might manifest itself in a relative lack of air time, financing, or attention toward the under-13s, as we place a stronger emphasis on those ages 14-plus, the youth, and student-age groups, unwittingly indicating that children have to grow up into teenage-hood to be considered worthy and useful. If this is true, it's comparable with the Greco-Roman culture's view of childhood—a period to be endured and to proceed through as quickly as possible so that you become useful to society as a grown man or woman.

Action/Declaration

If the Holy Spirit convicts you of this point, speak out and pray out loud the opposite of this assertion—that you are so glad to have children around—that you do and will welcome children. Read aloud the words in Matthew 18:5: *"And whoever welcomes one such child in My name, welcomes Me."* There is power in our declaration and our words, so decide to speak just those very words. Welcome every and any child you next see in your church community. Do all you can to allocate resourcing fairly to the youngest in your church and to offer this area of ministry your love and support. Recent statistics from the 4 to 14 Window organization revealed that in the United States, 27 percent of church populations were made up of children, yet their own children, in addition to giving to children overseas, received only 3 percent of church budgets.[66]

2. We repent of believing that we have nothing to learn from children.

Explanation/Clarification

This is actually confessing the sin of pride, thinking you know more than these little ones. You may know more because you have *learned* more head knowledge, but when we recall that Jesus said in Matthew 18, *"belonging to such as these is the kingdom of God,"* do we really know everything there is to know about the Kingdom? Confessing this erroneous belief allows you to make way to learn from little children and to appreciate afresh the attributes they possess which God loves: their sincerity, humility, naivety, vulnerability, and simplicity. The attitude that "we teach, you learn" creeps into our spiritual education programs surprisingly easily when we teach stories, write quiz questions, and feel proud that we have taught well when the right answers are shouted out.

Action/Declaration

Confess pride. Ask God to give you fresh understanding of what it means to come to Him as a child. Pray for your church family to look again on God's greatness with the eyes of a child. Share stories with one another and in public services of children's experiences with God. In worship, allow children unhindered opportunities to worship God in a way that celebrates their innocence and lesser years.

3. We're sorry for the times when we have not allowed children to express ideas and opinions.

Explanation/Clarification

Because children are fully-fledged human beings, they have thoughts and questions that deserve air time. They have opinions that matter. They may want to choose from a selection of activities; they may want to ask questions about why you say something; they may have an idea that they want to tell you about. Even if you think an idea won't work, even if you think the question is a silly one, children deserve to be listened to, within set boundaries. I mention boundaries because many of us know of situations where children hijack a leader's prepared activities by getting them "off topic" for some considerable time, to make a plan of activities suited to their preferences! But on the other hand, we need to beware of a classroom approach that strictly follows: "I talk, you listen; no questions allowed because they are a distraction." Remember from Chapter 2—the *searching faith* phase means that we should expect and welcome questions.

Action/Declaration

Repent of any time when you have been aware that children in the church have not been allowed to express their ideas or ask questions. Pray for Sunday school teachers and parents—that they would be able to strike the right balance between allowing free expression and careful teaching and instruction. Thank God for the way children *do* ask questions, which show that they are moving forward in their journey toward *owned faith*.

4. We repent of seeing children as "bait," using them to gather in the adults.

Explanation/Clarification

Seeing children as the bait to obtain the real prize *could be* grounded in a deficit of Christ-centered love for children, ignoring the value of their unique place in the world that God created. God could have sent Jesus to this earth any way that He wanted, even as an already-grown 30-year-old man translated down to earth; yet God chose to come as a baby who transitioned (like us!) from childhood through to adulthood. The reason for this is simple—we read in Philippians 2 that Jesus chose the meek and lowly place to enter this world.

However, in my experience, we can enter inadvertently into this position by "using" children. Even reading this might upset some of us who are loving, godly Christians. It was never our intent. All we want is to grow our church and see the Kingdom advance, and the thought that we are stepping on or over some developing human persons in our genuine desire to do this is really disturbing to think of. The US researcher George Barna said in 2009:

> …very few churches go beyond seeing children's ministry as "bait" that enables them to land the real treasure—i.e., adults. We spend roughly 68 times more money per capita on caring for the average felon than on a church's ministry to a spiritually hungry child.[67]

Action/Declaration

If you sense this *has* crept into the life of your church, take time to repent of this attitude. This could very well be one of the keys to release blessing on your children and family ministry. God treasures each little one and wants them to know more and more of Him. Without evangelistic strategies, many won't hear; and without nurture, many won't grow. Innate spirituality withers and dies without tending, and the "veering off" and away from God will surely happen.

After offering your repentance for this attitude, speak out your desire and intention to offer the Good News of Jesus unhindered to children in ways that are appropriate to them. Identify some key people, gifted communicators to the younger age groups, and resolve to place in their hands all that they need to allow this to happen.

5. *We're truly sorry for undervaluing these precious ones. We recognize that You, Jesus, lifted up the young and weak.*

Explanation/Clarification

This is closely linked to the previous point for repentance. Our churches in the West can, at times, struggle with valuing children for who they are. We may not have the same inherent need for children. We can "do church" quite professionally without their input or contribution. We don't have to spend time homeschooling children (unless we choose to, of course), as full-time education is provided. We don't even need to play with children so much in a hands-on way as there is so much to plug them into. Even real-life friendship and "hanging out" is rapidly being replaced by social media, which children as young as seven are rapidly becoming adept at using.

Children are *here* but not "needed" for our family's essential survival and well-being in the same way as other cultures. We are so used to doing things for ourselves, in isolation in an individualistic society, that we have lost that sense of *team* that we outlined in Chapter 3. Put simply, I think a Western worldview by default undervalues children—without meaning to. So many of us feel the tainting effect on us as we take time out to reflect and consider what has very insipidly snuck into the Church.

Mike Booker and Mark Ireland state:

> In some larger churches which run a wide range of activities, children's work can be viewed as a lower priority than "adult" activities like small-group leadership, eldership or preaching. Our society suffers from a strange type of snobbery which accords higher status to those who have least opportunity to influence people. Put at its starkest, a university lecturer (who works with people whose characters are already formed) is accorded higher status than a primary school teacher (working with people who may be far more open to change), who is in turn viewed as more important than a nursery nurse (who may have the potential for the greatest influence of all three). Seeping into churches, such an attitude means that work with children is undervalued and sometimes left in the hands of less able leaders. Children's work is for the beginners, so the

accepted wisdom seems to believe, adult leadership for the wise and mature.[68]

Challenging words. They speak of an undervaluing of children and the work amongst children, both in its shape and form and of those who do it. As I write these words, I too have defaulted at times to thinking of adult converts "worth more" than children. Lies! And that younger and more inexperienced people should be involved with children's ministry for "it's an easy place to start." This isn't true either! In many ways it's the hardest area to start as I believe a wide skill set is needed and children figure out frauds pretty quickly. The greatest potential to influence and instruct comes not from working with adults but with children. We could yet see a nation transformed from raising a generation who will not love their lives as much as they love Jesus Himself. What an honor and a privilege to shape!

Action/Declaration

Repent of this attitude and ask God to replace it with a fresh way of seeing children. It might be helpful to read out loud some Scriptures that speak of the value of children, such as Psalm 8:2, 34:11, 103:13; Matthew 21:15; and Mark 10:13-16. Look also at Scriptures about the poor, the weak, and lowly being chosen, such as the verses in First Corinthians 1:27-31.

Ask God to entrust to you and your church opportunity after opportunity to win, nurture, shape, and release young disciples. Believe that He will do this when unconditional, positive regard, and action toward children is in place in your faith community.

6. We're sorry that we spend less time and effort in preparing for teaching and talks to children.

Explanation/Clarification

In many churches, most weeks, the Bible is used in some way with children. It is read, taught, and discussed. Perhaps it's watched in some visual form. Evangelical Christians would agree that it is central to all that we do with children. And yet, I have seen a worrying trend to spend less time preparing "because it's for children." We can tend to segregate the teaching for children and adults, not just physically, but sometimes also in our attitudes to those we are teaching and for what purpose. Martin Luther said:

> When I preach I regard neither doctors nor magistrates, of whom I have above forty in the congregation, I have all my eyes on the maidservants and on the children. If the learned men are not well pleased with what they hear, well, the door is open.[69]

Luther considered the Word of God to be of utmost relevance to those whom society would prefer to ignore, but for him, their engagement with his teaching was his uppermost concern.

Action/Declaration

A survey of preaching friends, plus my own experience of preparing sermons, revealed that the *average* 35 to 45-minute sermon required *ten to fifteen hours* to prepare. I am not suggesting that preparing to teach children from the Bible requires that amount of background reading and research, but I am suggesting that a quick read-over of the passage and a ten-minute study the night before is not enough.

If we believe that God's written Word is powerful and active, then we must let it speak to us and work on our hearts before we presume to teach anything about its truths to anyone else, young or old. To get rid of unhelpful underlying beliefs…repent of them. Seek to uphold the importance and centrality of the Bible to *all* ages within your church—not just adults. Ask God to move in power following the teaching of His Word amongst your church's children. I believe He is longing to do this in greater measure.

7. *We repent of our irritation when children squirm or make noises in church.*

Explanation/Clarification

It's very common to be bothered by the antics of children. Children *are* noisy at times! A child might shriek or cry during a quiet moment in the service or during a long prayer. You may feel it is disrespectful; or you may feel annoyed at the parents for not taking the child out of the meeting room, and you may feel you are justified in your annoyance. It's not sin to be *tempted* to think like this—some shrieks and cries can be quite loud!

Children are not like adults. They can't sit still for long periods. They are made to move around and make noises. They talk to one another, ask questions, express joy, move their limbs. Yet 21st-century children are increasingly being forced into a passive adult-shaped mold (that perhaps not every adult fits into?) with a specific time "slot" chosen just for them in church. If they are part of the whole congregational gathering for a time, we may plan to have a "kid-friendly" song or a children's talk, delivered by a well-meaning staff member or volunteer, who often has no training on how a child's faith develops or his/her need to *experience* the things in the Bible as well as hear or read about them.

This is often the reason why some churches provide separate activities for children and adults from start to finish of the gathering. I have already outlined some of the reasons why this may not be the best plan of action for ongoing discipleship and family support. Children need to learn from us, and we need to learn from them. It's a short step to providing "infotainment," which threatens children's opportunities to learn from others more mature in the Christian faith.

Action/Declaration

Decide not to become annoyed. Ask God to place in you an attitude of thankfulness and gratefulness that there are children in your church. Someone once said, "I'd be worried if I *couldn't hear* any children." There are churches without a single child or teenager in them. Without children, the church as we know it will perish.

Repent of any times when you know you have been annoyed and perhaps even been glad when a certain child/baby has not been present. Remember that this was not Jesus' experience. He welcomed children. Speak this welcome out over your church's children, maybe under your breath as you gather each weekend!

Ask God to reveal in you any religious attitudes such as those seen in Matthew 21:15. Jesus had just healed the lame and the blind in the temple courts, had performed wonderful miracles, and children were shouting out praise, but the Pharisees were indignant.

8. Forgive us for being so quick to judge other people's parenting style because of their children's behavior.

Explanation/Clarification

We often begin to resent other people when their children exhibit behavior we don't like in church! Yet we should not judge or we will be judged too. R.T. Kendall says: "judging people is elbowing in on God's exclusive territory."[70] Warnings not to judge are given twice in the New

Testament—in Romans 12:19 and Hebrews 10:30. It's simply not our position to judge, as it is God's and God's alone.

Action/Declaration

Repent of the sin of judgment and determine to present an opposite spirit to the circumstances. For example, if a parent is struggling with their young children at church, sit next to them. Can you help them in any way? Bouncy little children sometimes just need someone to play peek-a-boo with them. This is not an unspiritual act! Smile and talk to the child(ren); tell them you are so glad to see them; and show pleasure that they have come to worship today. I have witnessed "challenging behavior" smooth out almost overnight when simple affirmation and positive words are spoken over the child and the family.

9. We're sorry for the times when we prevent children from experiencing God taking hold of their imaginations.

Explanation/Clarification

If we are parents or Sunday school teachers reading Bible stories to small children, helping our older ones with their Bible and prayer time, or pastors delivering children's talks, we are always aware of the pressure of time. At home we have only so much time to spend on Christian input. At church, we have only so much time for the singing, only so much time to deliver the children's talk before the sermon, only so much time before the next part of the service. In both the home and church sphere, the temptation to move quickly is huge for those of us who multitask, manage, and direct. Yet we need to slow down. Children of all ages are able to do something that I find incredibly challenging—they are able to "enter right in" to a story and experience it very deeply. Their emotions can be aroused in ways which we have forgotten. Imagination is a powerful tool for growing faith—the root meaning of the word is the "power of forming."

Action/Declaration

You may feel the Holy Spirit convicting you on this very point, of rushing, maybe not deliberately, but not slowing down sufficiently to give children time to experience Bible stories. Perhaps you have not allowed or have discouraged "wasted" moments of silence for children to ponder, permitting them the opportunity to imagine what the people in the stories were thinking and feeling. As we saw in Chapter 1, studies in children's spirituality recognize that they possess an intuitiveness that adults can easily dismiss; in other words, children can pick up the depth and the prophetic significance in Bible stories that we might think is way beyond them. "Godly Play"[71] does the exact opposite from many traditional models of teaching and allows time and space for awe, wonder, and imagination. It does not give children set answers but allows them time and space to "enter into" the stories and experience something of the mystery of God. Make space for wonder!

Wonder…attracts us with irresistible force toward the object of our astonishment.[72]

Say sorry to God for preventing children from using their imaginations, if you feel it's appropriate to do so. Determine to allow children space to experience God. You might remind yourself what they are capable of and do a little research on godly play. Its structured, liturgical approach will not suit everyone, but there are huge amounts to learn from it; its basic premise is that children are spiritual beings designed to have spiritual experiences which are initiated by God. Children deserve to have—*need to have*—experiences with God, because telling a whole load of stories with heavy emphasis on head knowledge is simply not working and is not keeping children in our churches.

In Chapter 7 we will look a little further at allowing children space to experience God.

10. We repent of our expectation that children should learn about God in the way we prefer.

Explanation/Clarification

William Glasser, an eminent psychiatrist with a particular interest in education, is attributed as the author of the following quote:

We learn…

- 10% of what we read,

- 20% of what we hear,

- 30% of what we see,

- 50% of what we see and hear,

- 70% of what we discuss,

- 80% of what we experience,

- 95% of what we teach others.[73]

It has proved impossible to find scientific proof of these statistics or the origin of this quote. It's poetry that contains wisdom to guide our thinking. So I shall use it as such, as I think it contains truth. Think about how you run activities and services in your church. Are they heavily reliant on speaking and listening? How do you disciple others? I suspect we often default to reading (books), listening to sermons/talks, or maybe watching DVD clips to help cement teaching points. We tend to get into one style of teaching and stick with it. So we may be a preacher who uses words only without any visuals. Or a groupwork facilitator who likes nothing more than to get people to "discuss with your neighbor." We all have different styles and preferences of how we teach and how we like to learn, so the best advice I can give to those of us teaching children and young adults is to offer variety.

Look back to point #9; does your work with children allow them to experience God's power, His majesty, and His holiness? Is there space for silence, to wait before God? Experiencing God's power and presence just once is worth a hundred readings of the story of Moses meeting with the Lord on Mount Sinai, because it brings the Bible alive. It reinforces to the child that this is truly *real*. She or he has heard it read from the Bible, received answers to questions on it, watched you live it out, sung about it, made something creative about it, but has now *felt it to be true for him/herself.*

Action/Declaration

Repentance is needed if you have become aware that you or your team are deciding how children will learn in ways that suit the adults or in ways that restrict children. Perhaps you might lay that down today, asking God to give you wisdom and sensitivity to allow children to experience Him unfettered and unhindered. Ask the Holy Spirit to show you how children love to respond to God in many ways, and make deliberate space for that to happen.

In the light of Chapters 3 and 4, if your children learn about God in a child-only environment, perhaps you might consider times where intergenerational worship and teaching might happen, where children and adults minister to one another? Subsequent chapters will outline some ideas on taking this forward.

11. We're sorry for not allowing children to express emotion in church, such as joy, sadness, and excitement.

Explanation/Clarification

Adults in the Western Church do not, by and large, manifest extreme emotion, be it joy, sorrow, or excitement. But we do seem to have transferred this expectation onto children, who can be exuberant and sorrowful within the same hour! Have we grown suspicious of emotion, that very thing we were created to manifest, as part of life in a community?

Some years ago, my husband and I were leading worship with about a dozen children in quite a traditional setting. We taught the children a little about the significance of Jesus' death on the cross and what it meant for us today. As soon as we started to sing, there was an incredible sense of God's presence in the room. I gently explained to the children that although we couldn't see Jesus, He had given us the gift of the Holy Spirit to help us know He was real, and it was His presence we felt. We quieted ourselves, singing a very simple song of adoration. All the children had their eyes closed, many had their hands out, and one was kneeling. One boy of about eight started to weep gently. Was he upset? No. He was experiencing God's powerful, manifest presence in a way he hadn't before. Did I panic and think, *A boy's crying!* (or worse still, *What will his parents say?*) No. I recognized God's presence and let him be. It was a sweet time and was an example of my expectations being blown away. A traditional setting, mixed age range of children, a short limited time, no "working up" period with a big band belting out songs—just two adults and one guitar, but God was surely among us.

Action/Declaration

Ask God to show you any times where you have shushed a child, or frowned at their joyful noise. How do you feel about children feeling sorrow? Maybe you have previously associated tears with a child being hurt, upset, or frightened?

Repent of any desire, deliberate or unintended, to control how children respond, and ask God to release deep spiritual experiences to children, which will stay with them all their days and show them something of the majesty of God.

On Good Friday of the year 2011, during family devotions (we had read from the Book of John, watched some of the "Jesus Film for Children" and sung together), my eight–year-old son wept and wept inconsolably as he realized what Jesus had gone through on the cross—for him. The realization that our sin separated us from God and that Jesus chose to die to take that sin away hit him hard. I held him and hugged him, but I didn't say, *"Don't cry."* I let him cry and assured him of my love for him and God's incredibly deep love for him. After a while, he went to his room (still crying) to have some quiet moments alone. After a few minutes, I went to see how he was. He had stopped crying and said, *"An angel spoke to me and told me not to worry; Jesus didn't stay dead, He's alive!"*

He had a spiritual experience that arose through his experience of deep sorrow. He had a spiritual experience that went far deeper than knowing the story. He knows that Jesus is alive and has loved him unreservedly since he was very small. He regularly repented (said he was sorry) for the things he did wrong or independently of God. But on that day, he understood the consequences of sin in a new and profound way. He didn't become a Christian "for the first time" on Good Friday, because he already loved Jesus with all his heart before that day. Rather, he had a spiritual experience that brought him further on in his journey of faith. We all have and need moments in our lives where we come back to the cross. And I can't help but think that not making room for emotion prevents such experiences from happening.

12. Forgive us for the times we've been glad that children have left the service—when we've felt that worship can truly begin.

Explanation/Clarification

It's particularly important with this point to stress that I am not referring to the general sense of relief we might feel when our own children or the corporate body of children have gone off to Sunday school. In my last church, after about 25 minutes in worship of all ages together, it took between five and eight minutes for up to 150 children to exit for their age-specific group time. The sense of relief as the children left was clearly palpable in the air. This wasn't sinful in itself! What we may wish to examine carefully is the times where in our own lives we have felt that children's presence is hindering us from receiving from God, or where we feel that real worship can begin. I was in a service once where the worship leader said: *"Once the children have left us for their groups, we will begin our time of worship."* I don't think it was meant to come out the way it sounded, but I am sure such words only reinforce unhelpful stereotypes of children, when my experience is of avid, hungry young worshippers who want to be with you and learn from you and show you their experience of God.

With that in mind, in Matthew 21 we read of Jesus' triumphal entry into Jerusalem. We come across some incredible insights in verses 15 and 16. The children in the temple courts were shouting, *"Hosanna to the Son of David."* This is the shout the crowds had made as Jesus approached the city. Remember the context of this passage and the status of children in Greco-Roman culture; they were not very important and were not key people involved in temple worship. In fact, they were probably waiting outside for their parents.

In Matthew 21:10-11, the shouts "Hosanna to the Son of David" took place *outside* the city. In verse 10, we notice that the people in the city were asking who Jesus was. They saw Him as a prophet from Galilee, yet the children in the temple courts cried out His name using His lineage, which was very important in Judaism, as we learned in Chapter 3. It indicated where you had come from, your status coming out of your heritage. Jesus the King!

Judith Gundry, Professor at Yale Divinity School, says:

> Children are not mere ignoramuses in terms of spiritual insight in the Gospel tradition. They know Jesus' true identity. They praise Him as the Son of David. They have this knowledge from God and not from themselves.[74]

Children saw Jesus as God's Son before other people realized who He was. And they saw Him as one to be praised, and that praise was loud, spontaneous, and natural. Children received a revelation of who Jesus was; yet their praise annoyed the religious teachers, and their cries were offensive to the priests. Jesus then quoted words from Psalm 8 to the indignant priests and teachers – words they would have known well. The Church needs to be really careful today not to fall into the same pattern.

Action/Declaration

Remembering that a sense of relief (when children leave the service to go to their own groups) is not in itself sin, ask God if there are any unhelpful attitudes that have been expressed in your church that you should bring into the light that God shines on our lives. I sense it is a very important attitude to renounce and leave behind. Children's worship opens something up. I have witnessed some incredible things happen when children are free to truly worship, which has a special effect on the adults who are present. It's one of the main reasons that I feel compelled to advocate times where we worship all together, not just as a token gesture for adults to "see the children."

There is a purity in children's worship that touches us at a deep level, and I believe spurs us on to connect more of ourselves with our Creator. To worship as a *child* means to laugh, cry, dance, shout, whisper, run, or kneel (in short: total freedom!) out of heartfelt praise and worship that is directed only toward a great God.

Children and worship are further discussed in Chapter 7.

13. For those of us who lead children's groups, we repent of seeing ourselves as baby-sitters.

Explanation/Clarification

This attitude can creep in to the hearts of those of us who look after children. I have spent many years overseeing ministry to a few hundred children in two churches, and it's hard sometimes not to feel that you are missing out when your colleagues or other members of the church talk about the dynamic things that have happened in this or that meeting. It's difficult not to feel a bit left out if no one asks how the youth Bible study went that morning, or asks about the children's program that day. But we have to couple this with the fact that we serve the Lord, not other people. We know we need His affirmation, not affirmation from others.

Yet no other area of ministry can leave us feel as much like baby-sitters, in a position of *statutory* responsibility (in that, if something went awry, we are actually responsible for the health and well-being of the child at that moment). I know from pastoring my volunteer teams that I need to pour love and affirmation into them, not because they constantly need flattery to feel part of the team, but because they are ministers to the youngest, and deserve to be honored and encouraged by me for what they do. My deepest hope and prayer behind this book is that you would feel affirmed and refreshed by the Lord Himself for the vital, discipleship-building ministry that you undertake. That if you are a parent, you are deeply encouraged in your part of nurturing and discipleship. That if you are a minister, pastor, or leader, you feel reinvigorated in all that you and your church do to reach children and families. *You are not, and never will be seen by God as hired help. You are tending the young in the flock under His care, and He cares for them tenderly and deeply.*

Action/Declaration

If you have ever felt like a baby-sitter, repent of this and allow the Lord to fill you afresh to minister to the young, fully equipped *in Him* and *by Him* to do so. Ask Him for renewed expectation for what He will do amongst the children's lives, and remember that you are having an input into world-changers. Lifelong behaviors and beliefs are developed during childhood and early adolescence. What an honor it is to partner with parents in the context of the church family to see these young ones shape the generations that come after them!

14. We're sorry too for our lack of encouragement to those who work with children. Lord, help us to value them more.

Explanation/Clarification

We all are guilty of not praising or encouraging people as well as we might, so please don't judge yourself too harshly! It's also true to say that there are many areas of church life where faithful servants are not given as much encouragement as perhaps some others are. I don't mean to write this point simply because I think children's ministry volunteers need to be encouraged. I write all of these words in this chapter with one aim only—to share with you what I feel I have to do to "make ready." I think this point for repentance is here to allow those of us who possibly face a *perpetual chronic shortage* of volunteers or burned-out staff members to consider whether this may be something to be addressed. I don't think there is any condemnation in saying sorry for the times when we know we have forgotten to encourage those who look after our youngest and to ask God to help us remember to do so– all around the church!

Action/Declaration

As outlined above, if you sense this applies to you, go for it. If there is a continual exodus of leaders from your children's ministry, it might be worth asking some of the individuals to be honest and tell you what caused them to leave. Of all the churches who contact me for help and advice, nearly every one of them cites discouraged and demoralized children's leaders as a major issue. Chapter 9 will offer some practical ideas on how to support the team.

15. We repent of the belief that resources and facilities are more important than the hearts of the leaders toward children.

Explanation/Clarification

As we saw in Chapter 1, the look and feel of the physical space *are* important in children's ministry, but there can come a point when achieving the right look and the right space becomes more important than the heart toward children.

I recently remembered that some pastors of growing churches had privately shared with me that this attitude caught them unawares. They had been genuinely encouraged about growth, and in the excitement of catering for this, perhaps by bringing new technology in and extending premises, something of the pastoring of volunteers' hearts easily slipped away. The attitude became, "as long as we have enough leaders to help us cater for growth," rather than accepting "fewer leaders who feel called of God to minister to our young."

Action/Declaration

If this resounds with you in any way, simply lay down the misplaced (and temporary) emphasis on buildings, equipment, or facilities, and ask God to bring a cleansing or re-prioritizing of the hearts of those involved with children. This is easy to sort, and I believe God is fully behind us getting this one right!

16. We repent on behalf of our church for anyone who works with our children out of any kind of wrong motives. Send us the very best, Lord.

Explanation/Clarification

I was slightly taken back when I felt this coming to mind to write down. I don't think the Lord was saying that our churches are full of people with sinister motives, but I did sense Him asking us to come to Him to repent *on behalf of* anyone who comes with *any kind* of wrong motives. This can take the form of wanting to work with children to avoid hearing the challenge that often arises when God's Word is preached, to the feeling that children provide a safe place from our own fear and pain, as well as the obvious predatory/sexual motive, which sadly, churches are not immune from.

I once read some advice to young men encouraging them to volunteer in the crèche or nursery, suggesting it was the ideal place to find a wife—because that was where they could find single women who wanted to eventually have children. But is this a biblical reason to volunteer to help? Is it preferring the needs of others (babies and toddlers) and serving with a Christ-like attitude, without any thought of what one will obtain in return? How would parents feel if the church nursery volunteers weren't primarily there to model God's love to their children, but to find something for themselves?

This chapter has been intended to allow us to rededicate everything we do with and for children and their families, and so like Solomon in Second Chronicles 6, there is a time to say, *"Hear from heaven and forgive the sin of your servants"* (2 Chron. 6:27).

Action/Declaration

Take time before God to do this. Allow Him to guide your prayers by His Spirit. Pray for pure motives for every person who comes into contact with children and young people in your church. Ask God to provide you the very best leaders.

I remember one year a team at our church was working with 8 to 11 year olds. The leaders were all female, and the children consisted of eighteen boys and four girls. Many of these boys lacked a Christian male figure in their personal lives. One evening we met to pray about this very issue which was really bothering us. We lay down all over my living room (ever since, that night has been known as "carpet night"!) and cried out to the Lord on behalf of those boys in particular and asked Him to send us the very best. Within six weeks, without any emotionally-loaded appeals in church, we had three fantastic male volunteer leaders. As I write this chapter many years later, they are still serving in children's ministry today.

God cares about who your children's ministry leaders are. I believe He cares very much about them because of His heart for children.

We ask that we, Your Church, would demonstrate Jesus' heart toward children. And we step away from everything that prevents that. Amen.

PART II

PRACTICAL ACTION

Chapter Six

WHOLE FAMILY DISCIPLESHIP

This chapter moves on to look at the topic of whole family outreach and discipleship—one which I am convinced our churches need to grasp as part of the process of "making ready" for what is to come.

Why is recognizing the entire family an important topic? Out of many possible reasons, let me suggest five:

1. For too long we have seen children in isolation.

We have recognized the fact that children are the most unreached people group in the world,[75] but they are incredibly easy to spot because they are found everywhere. Most evangelical churches usually engage in strategies to reach children to tell them the Good News of Jesus. Christians are involved in outreaches to children on the streets and in schools using a huge variety of methods. Yet what about the parents and grandparents? What about reaching the whole family?

The wonderful news is that great strides are being made in this area. Something is changing. For many years, Bill Wilson's Sidewalk Sunday School pioneered in this area by visiting each child and his or her family at home every week, providing practical support wherever possible to the whole family. In the United Kingdom, the Kidz Klubs around the country follow the same model.

Opportunities to engage with parents are increasing. As I outlined in Chapter 1, I feel as if something is stirring, that there is a fresh desire in parents to understand more about how their children are wired…and to be the best parent they can be. I have also observed a rising desire in churches to reach out to and support families. More and more, children's pastors and children and family workers are being appointed to work alongside the army of youth workers and youth pastors. This can be a double-edged sword, though. Having a paid worker *can* allow for fresh initiatives to happen in abundance, but I would caution that we need less of a "program" approach and more of an Old and New Testament approach to families (hence Chapters 3 and 4!). The church leadership team, and particularly those who teach and preach, still need to direct and guide the congregation on how to include and disciple the young.

2. In the United Kingdom, Europe, and the United States, we face a desperate state of affairs. Are we standing at the cusp of another great reformation?

We cannot remain complacent by simply assuming that the children we have already will remain. In both the United States and the United Kingdom, all evidence reveals that this isn't happening. In the year 2000 the church-going population of Great Britain was 4.4 million and 19 percent of this figure were children age 15 and under, or 836,000 children. By 2025 the church-going population is estimated to be 2.3 million with 5 percent age 15 and under, or 115,000.[76] That's a huge decrease in 15 years or so, if current projections continue. We will have lost 721,000 children in a 25-year period that we are almost halfway through.

If we were to go back to figures from the 1990s and compare them with the 2025 estimate, we will have lost contact with 1.1 million children.[77] We need to let these figures sink in without being frightened by a picture of gloom. There is hope. The UK researcher Peter Brierley says:

> Strategic action needs to be taken in the next ten years if this position is not to occur. It is no good waking up in 2030 and not liking what one sees; the opportunity to change that future picture has to be taken by 2015.[78]

In the United States, similar conclusions are being drawn, although it is not possible, nor correct, to directly compare the United States with the United Kingdom. In all but one (Hawaii) of the fifty states, church attendance is declining.[79]

But something is stirring and a reformation may be upon us that you have the opportunity to be part of. Professor Rebecca Nye has said:

Since the reformation, many emergent movements come from lone, marginal voices. Are we in the middle of a new movement or voice?[80]

There has been a child theology movement for a number of decades, and I have also seen a rise in its influence over recent years. I have watched the advent of movements like "Will You Make a Difference?" producing thought-provoking resources[81] for people to use in their local congregations. The 4-14 Window Organization[82] is another movement that started in 2009, and the Barna Organization[83] has been researching the religious influences upon children, youth, and families for many years now.

Negativity and decline are *not* the picture across the whole world. There are lessons to learn from churches in nations who are experiencing tremendous growth due to what I would summarize as *children contributing to and partaking in Kingdom practices—they are being discipled as naturally as drawing breath, through the input of the whole church*, which means they are learning to pray with expectant faith, worshiping and chasing the presence of God, and engaging naturally in mission which is marked by signs and wonders.

3. Discipling children and families is biblical.

In Chapters 2 and 3, we have examined the evidence that discipleship of the young was not outsourced, that *bet'ab* (the father's house), the clan, and the tribe in the Old Testament, and the *oikos*, the extended household of the New Testament, were places where instruction and remembrance occurred. It seems to me that this was a very natural part of life, and because of the emphasis on community or "team," each person within the community wanted to, and was instructed to, pass on the core beliefs and practices of their faith, love, and devotion to Yahweh, to those who were younger.

4. We must spend significantly more time and attention to discipling children and their families, because it is an area that is being ignored.

When I studied for my theology degree, one of my assignments was to audit the theological content of a range of resources in a category of my choosing. I chose to focus on published material that *discipled* children. Here's what I found:

Most devotional/educational resources in the United Kingdom and United States concentrated on…

- telling children *about* the Gospel.

- getting them *into* the Bible.

- telling children narrative stories *about* past or present-day heroes of the faith, or fictional stories about children and their families.

And there were some pastoral resources written for children dealing with difficult situations such as divorce and bereavement.

You will quickly see that this list focuses on the impartation of information—head knowledge. Thankfully this is beginning to change, but not fast enough and actually, a curriculum or book in itself is not going to bring about any type of significant change.

There are relatively few resources, possibly because Christians aren't always in agreement with the status of children before God, and because discipling children is not seen as an important area to write about (whereas, consider the vast number of books on church leadership!).

Some years ago, I listened to a mother testify to her new faith in Jesus and how He had helped her overcome many challenges from the past. She shared, with some considerable emotion and trembling, in a very public setting, that she didn't want her young daughter to go through what she had gone through. It was an dramatic moment. Immediately, God spoke to me and said, *"Many will come who are just like her. They will need your help."*

I knew, in an instant, that the *"your help"* in those words coming to my spirit meant *"us"*—the extended family, the clan, the tribe. We all are in this together, for the Kingdom. And it's not that hard a task. All that was needed was for this new family to be grafted into the faith community. My family spent time with this family during a meal. We helped with family devotions and provided some resources. The daughter then attended a kids' discipleship group, and one of the leaders spent additional personal time with her outside of the group. Her mother's small group leader supported her too.

My point in sharing this one example is that it isn't rocket science, but it does take some investment:

- of time.

- of money (to buy some age appropriate Bibles/reading notes).

- by more than just one person.

But it's worth the harvest that can be reaped—hurt and pain from a life lived without God's help can be avoided as in the case of that mother's dearest wish for her own daughter. Consequently, future generations who obey God, like she has, will live under blessing.

5. *Discipling children and their families results in natural mission.*

In concluding Chapter 4, I outlined my thoughts on discipleship and mission—that they go hand in hand. Children were present within the *oikos* as the church grew. All ages encountered the growing Christian movement and consequently came "under threat" (of conversion), as Pliny described, from the "Christian menace." I suggested in Chapter 4 that children played a part in missional activity wholly and completely alongside others in their faith community. So a very natural missional movement was born because whole families reoriented themselves toward Christ and welcomed others into this radical, but attractive, lifestyle.

I believe that children both then and now are naturally predisposed to being missional.

CHILDREN ARE A NATURAL CONDUIT

Children talk about God very naturally. Because they trust so easily, they also talk so easily about what they know and have seen and heard. This is not just simple mimicry; it is a God-ordained way of transmitting truth. I have no scientific proof for this, but I wonder if this ability is linked to the hardwiring in the brain to connect with God, identified by scientists and discussed in Chapter 1? They seem to have this natural ability to connect with God, to experience Him, and to simply tell others the truth about Him.

Let me give you an example. A three-year-old child is brought to a worship service by a family friend. The child's grandmother, who is her full-time guardian, remains at home. The fact that her grandchild attends Sunday school gives her a break for a few hours. As the weeks and months pass, her little grandchild tells her repeatedly that Jesus loves her, that Jesus forgives her for the things she does wrong, and that she can tell Jesus the things that are worrying her and He will listen. I believe this child is speaking directly into the things her grandmother most needs to hear at those moments.

Some months later, I have the privilege of sitting with this grandmother in her home as she shares some of the stresses in her life. She tells me what her grandchild has said and asks if this can be true—does Jesus really feel this way about her? She confesses how deeply impacted she has been by the little child's words to her. I am able to tell her that it is true and to pray with her and to encourage her to let go of some of the guilt she is carrying and to receive God's love for herself—all because of the insistent words of her three-year-old granddaughter.

There is another similar story but not with so positive an outcome. After our annual summer holiday club for children had ended, a brother and sister returned home, and for some months, they continued to sing the songs they had learned about Jesus' love, care, and protection. Even though they explained to their parents what the songs meant to them, the children were not allowed to return to the holiday club the following summer because their parents did not want the same thing to happen again. They were not comfortable with their children having this experience. Dear reader, all over our world children are speaking and singing the most incredible truth about the nature of God Himself! They do it innocently, naturally, and yes, sometimes like lambs to the slaughter. They need our love and support, care and protection. As such natural conduits, children are also susceptible to attack.

CHILDREN ARE MIGHTY WARRIORS

In 2005, I had a vivid dream. I watched as hundreds of terracotta warriors were unearthed, just like those uncovered in China in 1974. But these weren't adults; they were individual children, each armed with weaponry and precisely positioned in battle formation for the task that was ahead. I didn't know this at the time of the dream, but each terracotta soldier that had been uncovered from the Emperor's Palace in Xi'an, Shaanxi Province, was absolutely unique. No two soldiers of the eight thousand discovered were the same.

At the time of this dream, I felt the call of God to love, support, and equip children to stand strong in their faith. As a response to this picture in

2005, I wrote a vision statement which said to the church that we would disciple children to be victors, not victims. I knew from God that I could have high expectations, not just for the children in my church to perform, but high expectations of their capability of being *missional disciples*. In my discipleship of my own children, helping other parents with theirs, or personally teaching other children, I constantly reinforce that in everything God has given *to us* and done *for us*, He has *blessed us* and *shown His great love for us* as human beings, *that we might then share this Good News with others. Children "get" this so easily.*

I knew that I would not be alone in wanting to disciple children, that there would be many people in churches in the comfortable West with the same desire. And as the years have passed, I have found an increasing number of people feeling the same kind of compulsion across denominations, organizations, and countries. We are to get ready!

So first, I was to help children grow up knowing who they were in Christ so that they would be effective in missions, and second, as a result of this dream, I knew I was to help prepare the Church to be the *safe place*, the *covering* for these little warriors. I write this book asking all who read it to partner in this endeavor. These children aren't disciples-in-training; they are disciples who are experiencing the battle now.

When she was six years old, my daughter came home from school in tears because a boy in her class had laughed at her for believing in Jesus. "He's not real; He's dead!" she was told. This was devastating for my daughter, so what followed in our household was a crash course in apologetics suitable for six year olds in the classroom and the playground. I emphatically state that speaking confidently about the uniqueness of the person of Jesus in an antagonistic secular classroom is certainly being a missional disciple. Imagine every adult having the same confidence to stand strong for Jesus against influential peers who express ignorance about Jesus!

May every member of the Church of Jesus aid in this task of teaching, instructing, welcoming, and loving children but also with a keen eye to watch, protect, and intercede for them by name. They are not designed to operate as lone rangers but alongside others in their family, and as part of the clan and tribe of the people of God.

DISCIPLING CHILDREN AND ADULTS
IN CHURCH TOGETHER

Assuming that you agree that children can draw close to God through Jesus, what are the essential components to build into a strategy for growing our children's faith? In the following chapter, I will look at some key principles that allow us to build for growth in every way. While you may want to read that information right now, please stay with me here and consider the structural changes that first need to happen—the "ditch preparation."

In 1983, Larry Richards suggested "Five Processes of Spiritual Development," which nearly thirty years later are still relevant to the Church of today. What I want to suggest is rooted in this:

> Children need to be involved in processes that communicate belonging. Children must *feel* that they belong to their faith community, not just be told that they do. This belonging needs to be demonstrated through the policies and practices of the community. Forming good relationships with children is the responsibility *of all members of the community*, not just those who work with them in children's programs or in school (emphasis added).[84]

So here are some practices to consider which aim to bring children fully into the church family, to instruct them about the Lord's goodness and faithfulness, and to prepare them for mission.

1. Schedule times where children are present in worship services to witness baptism and communion.

How will children learn about the importance and the symbolism of the sacraments if they never see them happening because they are in another room? Instead of relying on Sunday school teachers to tell children about the sacraments, allow them to them see and hear for themselves—and perhaps to participate.

I do not intend to comment on children and baptism at this point due to respect for the different denominational backgrounds of our readers. I will say only that if children are able to know and love Jesus and want to put Him first in everything, might there be a way that we could celebrate that adoration in our churches?

Regarding communion, it might be helpful to think about how your church sees children with regard to the Lord's Supper.[85] I believe that children who understand the significance of Jesus' death and resurrection, who demonstrate their love for Him, are qualified to share in this most important act of remembrance. And so, in the two (Baptist) churches in which I have served as children's and family pastor, we have asked parents to talk with their children about the meaning and reason for communion, so that the children may receive the bread and the wine if their parents are agreeable for them to do so. Children are not present every time communion is given; however, our entire staff team works together to schedule worship services in which *everyone* is gathered together a few times a year for communion.

What of the children whose parents will not allow them to take the bread and the wine? This is not a reason *not* to talk about why we do what we do; rather, it's a reason to teach why and hear from the children themselves. And so I am able to pull together the children's thoughts or experiences on the Sundays when everyone is together. We have talked about the symbolism and asked children to share what it means to them (testimony time).

Your church's response to this issue has to be worked out under the authority of your leadership team of course, as you need to be unified and in one heart about your practices. I would never recommend forcing a practice you or your church leaders haven't thoughtfully and theologically reflected upon. My aim in Chapters 1 through 4 was to take us all to a point together where we see the importance of bringing children fully into the heart of our church community.

Over the years, some denominations have used catechisms, which are statements about core doctrines in the form of questions and answers, learned by rote. This is not a new invention—memorizing important information has been around since the early days of the church in the form of creeds, which a particular mark of Martin Luther's practices in the 16th century. He encouraged parents to cultivate their children's faith and thought catechizing was an effective means of doing so. He believed children were the most susceptible to formation. He was partly right, but unfortunately, and paradoxically for a reformer, this began to be applied with legalistic force, using quite extreme punishments for those who refused to study the catechism.[86]

Deuteronomy 6 (mentioned in Chapter 3) showed us that discussion and exercising the Christian principles and practices in all of our daily activity is a biblical model to follow. This allows for instruction in the context of familial love and acceptance, motivated by a desire for the absolute best for the other person. This does not mean that I am saying memorizing Scripture is wrong! However, we should not overemphasize cerebral learning—the power of recall—without similarly valuing actual experience.

2. Incorporate specific times of worship and teaching simple theological truth to all ages together.

In the United Kingdom, many churches from varied denominational backgrounds hold monthly "all age" or "family" services. On these days there is no Sunday school, Bible class, or children's church; everyone meets together in one gathering place. Yet many churches have given up on attempting to conduct these services, because it is so difficult to present instruction to all ages present. Could it be possible, though, that the enemy prevents a successful experience because it could be a key event for your church? Just my thoughts! Could it be that worshipping, listening to the Bible being read, and hearing some simple teaching from it, along with time to make a response to God, recapture something of the powerful gathering of community that we see examples of in the Old Testament? In Nehemiah 12:27-43, we read of women and children being part of the joyful celebration when the walls of Jerusalem were rebuilt. They were present at the procession of the choirs and fully understood the significance of the task that had been accomplished. Children were not shut away elsewhere while "important business" happened among the adults. God was worshipped by the *whole* community.

A suggested starting place is to ask, "What are we trying to achieve?" Why are you currently holding all-age services? If you are not holding any, what's preventing that from happening? Again, the purpose of this book is not to advocate that a leadership team must do x, y, and z, but to ask churches to reflect on *why* they do what they do and to consider what could change *if* we were to see more children and families come to faith in Jesus.

We are living in days when the shape of what we do must change. So often our mission has been driven by the way we do church, which means that we expect new people (of any age) to fit in to *our* structures, *our* service times, *our* ways of learning. Why not try a way of gathering together and learning that has historical biblical precedent and also has developmental advantages for growing in faith? It doesn't matter how old or young the person is, we all have things to learn from one another.

In a real-life example, a minister preaches a thousand sermons on how to have a worshipping heart, but it easily falls on deaf ears, crossed arms, and stony hearts. Yet, one after another, children read out psalms of praise that they have written to God their Father in and amongst the song worship (not as a performance where everyone listens politely but as part of the act of worship). Tears flow; hearts are stirred and opened up. We discover that if we are always separate, we miss out on so much.

There are many topics that we can teach in intergenerational settings that give us instruction, insight, and encouragement. I have no space to write about this subject in detail, but topics and themes that I have used in all-age services have included: God has chosen you; listening to His voice; remembering His faithfulness; God's loving-kindness; the importance of the Bible; His gifts are for today; care for the poor; God heals; have a heart of flesh instead of a heart of stone; He's with you in hard times; and more.

I have never used books or web resources to help me plan all-age services, preferring to ask the Spirit what He wants to underline to our community of believers at the present time. We want to move toward joining together at times, and believe that if we are in a season of something special as a church, that it is for every one of us and not just those ages 18 and over.

Prior to launching a teaching series, the senior pastor and I look at dates to schedule all-age services. Then I go away to think and pray about what we should do. We then get back together briefly and discuss our thoughts. Subsequently, I involve other people in putting the service together as we aim to stay close to the overall theme. It's important to me to consider what the adults have been and will be learning in the weeks before and after the all-age service, so it does not cause an "interruption" to the normal service.

For example, my former senior pastor taught a series called "Fly," regarding being spiritually free and full of God's Spirit. This series, taught to adults, lasted several weeks, and we also held an all-age service in the middle of that time entitled "Fly Gifted," in which I taught about the gifts of the spirit to everyone—all ages gathered together. It formed part of the main series, and like any other Sunday, people had the opportunity to come and receive prayer following the teaching from the Bible. How moving it was to see children and teenagers stand alongside their parents and all receiving prayer for a fresh infilling of the Holy Spirit!

I suggest the following six "essentials," which will prevent you from going down the "children's entertainment" route, which many all-age services run a risk of becoming. You might like to use it as a checklist.

Take time to plan for:

- *simplicity*—one overriding theme that connects all points on this list.

- *clear reading of and explanation of Scripture*—looking for simple theological truth to emphasize throughout the whole service.

- *worship* that is neither just "children's songs" nor wordy adult-only songs—that express something of God's character, lead people into the presence of God, and importantly, allow them to linger there.

- *visual stimuli*—media clips, drama, or dance.

- *telling stories*—testimonies by real-life people or using DVD clips that reinforce the power and reality of a life lived with God.

- *a time to respond to the Spirit in prayer and reflection and with ministry to anyone who wants to respond.* (Consider a variety of ways to respond—silence, kneeling, praying out loud, coming forward to take part in a symbolic act, receiving prayer.)

Some all-age services include a time where children make, color, or paint an artwork. While I have occasionally put this into practice, it's not included as one of the six "essentials." Dealing with large numbers of children, it's just not always possible. I have found "make, color, and paint" can sometimes be an excuse for not stepping out into the nerve-racking but exciting ground of the supernatural or unpredictable.

3. Establish times in your church life where children are present in smaller intergenerational gatherings—missional communities (see Chapter 8), prayer meetings, celebration times, or other intergenerational groups.

This strikes me as being absolutely vital. Are there some ways we can incorporate children into the life of the church so that they see and hear the things God is doing by using times of prayer and celebration that are separate from Sunday gatherings?

Church prayer meetings. To do this at our church, I proposed that we start the prayer meeting earlier and allow the first hour and a half to be given over to worship and prayer with all ages present, usually culminating in a time where children pray for adults and vice versa. A moving and powerful time! Each time this occurs, I teach on the need to repent and come to God with clean hands and a pure heart. Then I remind everyone present (all ages) that prayer is a two-way process: talk *and* listen; so in our corporate prayer times we should allow time to listen to God for encouraging words, pictures, and Bible verses for ourselves or to share with others. This setting is an ideal launch pad for practice and is especially affirming for new Christians and younger people.

Working in partnership with others who have become good friends, I have found that this model has developed into one I can use at events outside of the local church as well, such as Pray Any Way.[87]

Intergenerational housegroups. In Europe and North America, we have deferred mostly to holding midweek meetings at 7:30 or 8:00 P.M., thereby alienating children, teenagers, single parents, and certain seniors from being able to come to meetings because they are held in the evenings—another case of people having to fit in with *our* ecclesiology, our way of doing church. Not everyone wants to travel out in the dark to come to a distant church building. As an alternative, home-based meetings can be warm, welcoming, and flexible in meeting times. Some churches have established children's small groups or youth home groups, and while I have experience of managing both, let me focus briefly on a third option—intergenerational groups.

The pattern I have used involves a two-hour time commitment on Fridays, 6:00 to 8:00 P.M. or Saturdays, 4:00 to 6:00 P.M. (And it's important to stress that there is no requirement to stay longer than two hours if the objective of this kind of gathering is to meet a felt need and not simply replicate "church.")

One hour—share a meal together. If space is a pressure, allow the kids to eat first; then they can play while adults eat.

Second hour—gather everyone together, worship (perhaps using DVDs such as those by Doug Horley or Hillsong Kids), share in some interactive teaching, lead in some time for response, and pray for one another—children praying for adults and vice versa.

My research indicates that flexibility is vital. Your church model may be cell, G12, missional communities, attractional, or traditional (insert your own adjective!); but by using the biblical principles I have outlined thus far, ask the Holy Spirit to lead you into places where children and teenagers can join in the faith journey with adults who will encourage them and model a lifestyle to them. Regarding what to teach in these settings, there are very good resources from the Cell UK[88] and from the Joel Comiskey group.[89] Look for some of your best people to lead these kinds of gatherings, who will neither patronize children nor ignore adults, but who will lead all to the Father through Jesus in the power of the Holy Spirit.

4. Offer to run specific discipleship groups for children.

We often make sure that teenagers and adults who come to faith are followed up in some way. I gave an example earlier in this chapter of ways specific individuals can provide input into a new family who are desperate for help But what regular help do we give children in their normal, everyday living as a Christian?

My anecdotal evidence is that we default to teaching Bible stories without vibrant, experiential, practical application. One of the first questions you might have is, what resources should I use? It's not a sin to want to look at off-the-peg prepared materials, especially because we all are busy people. I would encourage you to first look at what topics you consider important to discuss with adults who are new to the faith and replicate them wherever possible! We may give children instructions on things *we* consider important (i.e., prayer, reading the Bible, and telling others); but do we teach our children how and why we worship, why we give away some of our money, and how we experience bad thoughts turning into good thoughts in our minds? What practical steps do we take when we are hurting deeply? What should our response be when people are unkind to us?

Two good friends of mine have written some of the United Kingdom's most recent discipleship material[90] for people who are new to Christian-faith.[91] I don't think there is a topic in the book (e.g., on identity, community, advancing the Kingdom, to name but a few sections) that I wouldn't want children and teenagers to have a good grasp of, so it gives me or anyone who disciples younger people a great base to work from.

A useful exercise for a leadership team to carry out is to audit whatever is used for discipling teens/adults and ask: what here is relevant to children? Are we giving material to our church's children that covers topics relevant to their age and stage of development? Do we know what *is* relevant? Consult with some teachers, parents, children's ministry team leaders, and pastors, and attempt to put together your own discipleship course, being mindful that the reason you do this is in preparation for more children to become part of your church family. Although written more for children's cell groups, have a look at the Living with Jesus series.[92]

Another great resource, unique as far as I am aware at the time of this writing, is Luke Into Jesus,[93] a book entirely dedicated to helping children understand the person and work of Jesus through the Book of Luke. This is precisely the kind of resource we need for the coming influx of children and families to the Church—people who have no prior knowledge of Jesus, helping us point the way over and over again to Him.

5. Share a high-level vision and teaching with adults.

Share the theology behind children's spiritual development, what the Bible says about *family*, not just families, and about inclusivity—*everyone* has a role. Talk about children's spirituality and about their ability to connect with God in ways adults can only dream of. Address the wrong and even harmful views of children that exist, that restrict, stifle and deaden their young spirits, but yet they will turn like flowers following the sun in response to the love and care of their heavenly Father. Stress the need to nurture and model faith.

This is not about teaching parenting skills; it is about helping *everyone* grasp what a biblical worldview is as opposed to a worldly one, that there are implications for every one of us in every area of church life.

Young people are being *brought to* church rather than actively discipled. In a wide-reaching survey in 2002, the Barna Organization found that less than one out of every ten church-going families reads the Bible or prays outside of family meals in a typical month. Fewer than one out of every twenty church families takes part in any worship activity outside the church service in a typical month. This is despite four out of five parents (85 percent) saying that they have the primary responsibility for the moral and spiritual development of their children.[94]

The very first time I read these statistics I found them shocking; but as I continued to ponder them, I realized that it made perfect sense and that I actually concurred with these findings. I would add that I've watched many families no longer attend church every week, but take on a pattern of attending two weeks out of four, or three weeks out of five. Of course discipleship is not all about attending worship services, but part-time attendance does result in fewer and fewer opportunities for the Christian faith to make an impact on the lives of children.

And of course, if the children are not present, or are inconsistent in their attendance, then other adults who are not their parents have less opportunity to have any kind of input into their lives—no kind words are received, no expressions of pleasure and encouragement are passed on, and wee ears don't hear the testimonies to the goodness of God or the feedback of answered prayer.

I am now realizing in greater measure as the years go by that this unintentional lack of action by many parents regarding non-Sunday spiritual input is one of the enemy's chief strategies to eradicate a natural missional force to be reckoned with. Never underestimate what emanates from children who love God with all their heart, mind, and strength and who have tapped into His reserves of love and power so that they can tell their friends and classmates.[95]

6. Involve a key carrier at the church leadership level.

It is vitally important that someone on the leadership team actively advocates for children and young people in the church. I don't write this as a children's and family pastor who is wielding an axe of bitterness! I have been incredibly supported in the two churches in which I have worked and have been entrusted with a huge amount of freedom and responsibility to see the children's and family ministry flourish. However, from feedback I have received from all around the country, this is one area we desperately need to address. Ministry staff and volunteer teams need to be actively supported by our leaders, not because we are needy and attention-seeking, but because we are the propagating seedlings that paradoxically are more able to move mountains than some adults! They have a part in the missional movement outward that will capture every age and stage of life.

George Barna advises senior pastors to choose to be strong advocates of ministries that are both strategic and influential while fitting within the boundaries of his/her church's unique vision:

> I believe that if the (senior) pastor does not include the ministry to children as one of the top church priorities, the chance of that ministry reaching its potential and having a significant impact on the lives of the church's children is severely reduced.[96]

I don't mean to single out senior leaders for attention over and above the importance of investing in volunteers. (Chapter 9 will review this point in more detail.) However, I wholeheartedly agree with the saying that you can go only as far as your leaders will allow you to go. I could have the most passionate, God-given vision for children in this coming revival, but I still need the support of, and to be cheered on by, my leaders and my church.

During my research for this book, I found a most interesting model of practice. At All Saints Worcester (an Anglican church in England), the vicar Rich Johnson has taught and modelled with intent that everyone is part of the family, and so all should share in the task of raising our children and honoring parents. He and his curate play their part as parents helping out *and* as group leaders in the children's church. His aim is to send a twin message: as an example to parents and as the vicar committed to children's ministry, not just "from the front." He establishes the Sunday preaching schedule so that once a month both he and the curate are not part of it. Instead, on that Sunday, the vicar leads and coordinates the children's team and one of the age-groups himself. I would point out that this is not a small fellowship. There are approximately ninety children involved, and in the UK context, this is a substantial number.

He is not operating a "one-man-does-everything" ministry, but has chosen to send a strong message, *through his actions,* about the place of children in the church's life. This is an example of a key carrier who is a senior leader, although I would add that not every pastor, minister, or leader has to personally run one of the children's teams in order to be a key carrier—but it does send a powerful message out that children are important.

Obviously, this case study is not transferrable to every context, and perhaps this program may change according to the vicar's limits of time as the church grows. But what kind of message do you glean from this picture?

Are we cultivating leaders who are "too busy" or "indispensable" on a Sunday to spend time teaching and modelling their own walk with Jesus to children? To model something to parents *and* children? Most ministers rate pastoral visitations to the elderly and housebound as essential; but how would they rate the time and attention given to the routine (not hospital emergency!) pastoral care of children and young people?

Dear readers, it's not my heart to ask these questions to be provocative purely for the sake of it, but because, as we saw at the start of this chapter, some of our denominations or churches might not be around in fifty years if we don't consider some kind of radical action. *Now* is the time to make changes, but we need our leaders to be the first to hear, act, release, and support.

7. Provide teaching to parents, for they are desperate for help and instruction in how to disciple their children in the ways of Jesus.

Many operate what Barna calls "twisted logic" which states:

> I know I am to be the number one person inputting into my child's spirituality but because I am not that great at it, I'll hand my child over...[97]

Despite 85 percent of parents believing that they are primarily responsible for their child's spiritual development, they also genuinely believe that the Church is better placed than they are to actually do it. This is perhaps an indicator of a much more serious issue and one that I simply want to flag for your consideration.

The Barna Organization examined born-again Christians and asked them what they held to be true in six areas:

Respondents were asked:

- Who do you understand God to be?

- What is your understanding of Jesus' life on earth? Did He sin?

- Is satan real or not?

- Do you believe that you can earn your salvation, or is that a free gift from God?

- What is your personal responsibility to share your faith with others?

- What do you believe about the Bible? Is it accurate or not?[98]

Based on the responses, the research showed that in the United States, *only nine percent of adults who profess to be born again* possess a biblical worldview. Does this matter? If we consider that a worldview shapes the choices we make, how we live our lives, and *how we bring up our children,* then it matters hugely. A biblical worldview is, put simply, *making choices with God and His Word at the center of our motivation, our thoughts, and our actions.* Therefore, it is imperative to run hard after a biblical world-view, for it affects everything we do, so that we are together in the task of thinking and acting like Jesus! Ask yourself, what kinds of things did Jesus do? And then pursue these things from the very youngest age and across the board in your church.

Teaching and modeling a biblical worldview is not just about correcting heresy; it's about a deliberate and rigorous effort to raise up disciples from the very earliest age. At the time of Barna's research (2003), *85 percent of born-again adults did not have a biblical worldview.*[99]

This unfortunate statistic concerns me greatly, and so, in the next chapter, we will be addressing ways to make dramatic changes.

Chapter Seven

BUILDING FOR GROWTH

UP, IN, AND OUT

UP, IN, and OUT is a helpful concept—our church vision and practice and our own personal walk with God should combine elements of all three. Jesus lived out His life in three relationships—with His Father, with His disciples, and with the world around Him.

UP refers to the relationship we each have with God through Jesus in the power of the Holy Spirit. I have written of young children's innate spirituality, their ability to connect with God, and the model I believe is laid out for us in the Old and New Testaments to spur one another further and deeper in relationship with a loving, holy God. I have also reinforced the need to teach children and young people that, in order to grow in relationship with God, they must repent of their sin and walk daily in a relationship that puts God first.

IN refers to our need to build one another up, disciple one another, and create communities that ensure that no one is excluded.

OUT refers to the fact that we live in a world that, for the most part, does not accept or engage with a loving God. Therefore, we are the called-out people of God (*ekklesia*), sent out to bring transformation in every way to the world—to individual people, to communities, and to nations.

As the Introduction to this book briefly outlines, my life story to this point so far has been an inseparable intertwining of the UP, IN, and OUT. Through the deepest moments of enjoying the presence and power of God, I have always been left with a deeper desire for others to know just how good He is. I have felt compelled to do so. I have been deeply sorry for the times where I haven't modeled this as well as I might have, but that doesn't stop me from waking up each morning wanting to do the best I can with the help of the Holy Spirit.

In this chapter, I want to introduce some of my own personal non-negotiables that ensure that children and their families are prepared well to be part of a great move of the Church outward. I have mentioned the three simple words UP, IN, and OUT so that as you read through this chapter, you might make a mental note when each of these three topics are being covered.

Set the Bar High

Set the bar high in your expectations as an adult.

It is my belief that every age and stage of life, although full of challenges and not immune to hardship and suffering, is to be lived through a lens of "life to the full" (see John 10:10). No one stage of life is "better" than another in terms of fruitfulness (which I will interpret here as being used by God); yet sometimes we are desperate to gallop through one stage of life to get to the next. This is where the "if only's" can rob us of what is actually ours to walk into. I don't read in Scripture that bearing fruit is only for those who have everything altogether, or who are over age 40, or who are single young adults. Bearing fruit that will last is for everyone who loves and follows Jesus (see John 15:16).

I prayed recently with one young mother who was sad about what she felt she was unable to do in terms of mission and ministry. And yet this is *precisely* the age and stage of life where we have incredible opportunities to establish our beliefs and experiences of the Kingdom of God not only into the lives of our own children *but also* into the lives of other young parents who are not yet Christians, who worry about their children in this world full of risk. We have an open door to not just speak truth, but to actively *live out* our faith that makes us different.

Let's set the bar high and have an expectation that we will each come into contact through our natural networks (*oikos*) with "persons of peace" (see Luke 10:5-7), those who are open to us and welcome us to be part of their lives in some way. This will be as true for the elderly follower of Jesus living in a retirement community as it is for a child who knows how much Father God loves him/her when they are at school. *Set the bar high in your expectations for children and teenagers.*

Children and teenagers can also bring the Kingdom of God to earth, when, like adults, they are walking in a relationship that seeks to put Him first. They can and *do* pray for friends who are sick, tell stories of God's protection during bad dreams, and look out for and serve people who are friends with them. Their friends' families may become "persons of peace" that your whole family will have an opportunity to love and serve.

As our young children become teenagers, we adults have less contact with the other parents we had met and spent time with on social outings, at play groups, or at school functions. Yet we don't want to lose our missional edge if we become embroiled in other well-meaning activities that take up a lot of our time. And so, I want this chapter to encourage and inspire you to look at all the ways your own family or others view church and their responsibility to tell others. *Make time* for serving others.

There is an example of a school class of Chinese children in Wanderlust Production's *Finger of God* DVD, sent there by non-Christian parents so that the children would receive a good (moral) education. The narrator goes on to say that *"most if not all of these children will lead their parents to Christ."* As I wrote in Chapters 4 and 6, children are natural missionaries. They say what they see, and they demonstrate what they know.

I've watched several parents come into relationship with God because their children talked and talked with passion about the exciting God they had encountered at summer holiday club (or vacation Bible school). For some parents I know, it was less about the Christian event we had invited them to, and more about what they saw and heard in their own children.

And so, I want to encourage the Western Church to cheer on our younger generations as they live their faith out in school, one of the hardest places to be a Christian. I believe this isn't just so that the young people will feel loved, but because we have a responsibility as we play our part of the Old Testament team concept.

SEE CHILDREN AS GOD SEES THEM

In Jesus' description of what belonged to children (see Mark 10:14), He stated that they clearly possess an ability to manifest the Kingdom in ways that we may have long laid aside. Yet I think their simple faith and trust can rub off on us. I have been changed by being around a child's hunger to know and experience more of God. I agree with Keith White's view that we should consider children, their characteristics, and the contribution that they bring to the church community, as *essential to understanding the way of the cross and the kingdom of Heaven*. He states that Jesus, the little child placed in the midst, and the kingdom of Heaven are a triad.

Each part of the triad illuminates the other two; in welcoming or receiving one, the other two are also accepted.[100]

I consider it an absolute privilege to oversee what is happening in the lives of children, because:

- I am drawn to what they see and experience of God.

- I believe they demonstrate sheer dependence as recipients of the Kingdom of God.

- I believe God wants to restore this again to our faith communities.

- I believe that in these coming days children are pivotal in the conversion and reorientation of many households toward Jesus.

Everything that Jesus did was to point the way to His Father, to demonstrate what the Kingdom looked like. And I think that children may have a very key part to play in this purpose. A close friend who is an Anglican vicar sent an email to me after I had shared the vision for this book with him. I think he has summarized what I believe is coming:

God is going to build a new generation of leaders out of our current children who will have a faith birthed and founded in kingdom power and presence first. Understanding will be important but it will not be received as an "apologetic" to initiate faith, instead it will be discovered as an explanation of the reality encountered. Grown alongside years of seeing God at work, living and active.

...for too long we have drawn people to the faith by argument, rational discourse and presentation of the doctrines. We have sought to offer a metaphysic in the hope that people would like the sound of the Jesus "philosophy" and choose to live it out. But Christianity is a "fact" in search of an explanation and is always at its most vibrant when an encounter with the reality of the Divine provokes an individual to ask, "what does this mean?" For children so often their faith is birthed in the simple acceptance that God is real, not just a good idea. The new Church birthed in our children will be built on signs and wonders, acts of power and not by persuasive words. We will be running to catch up with them.[101]

I do believe a reformation is coming, and this book is all about preparing for that! To start developing the ideal conditions to train and equip those who are new to the faith (of any age), make sure your church's ministry is prepared by following the suggested key principles.

Key Principle 1: Knowledge and Experience Are Needed

Ivy Beckwith writes:

Generation Y is experience-oriented. These kids find meaning and value in immediacy and in living in the moment. Their mantra for life and learning is "I want to try it." Only then will they decide if they like the experience or not....They want to use all their senses as they learn, and they want their learning environments to provide experiences, not just facts and formulas. They want to do in order to learn. And when it comes to experiencing a spiritual life—and they are spiritual people—they want to experience God, not just learn about God. They don't just want to be entertained (emphasis added).[102]

In Chapter 2, we considered the inadequacies of basing all of our discipleship on pure information transfer (head knowledge only). So every time I gather children together, in the sung worship time, or during Bible time, or in response times, whenever I look for opportunities to try out and do the things we have read and talked about. There are many experiences you can incorporate into your learning time. Kneel. Lie down in God's presence. Try using smells sometime! Pray for anyone who is ill. Give to someone who has a need. Draw, paint, or write down what you hear God saying. Use your voices loudly to lift God high or to shout

out spontaneous prayers to see a breakthrough come. Break demonic power in Jesus' name.

Whether you are a parent, relative, friend, or leader, my advice is to *release* and *not force*, and *model* the experiential yourself. But be real to who you are, and lead with integrity. Relax about your own experiences, or lack thereof. God will make up for any deficiency you may feel you have, if you have an open, teachable heart. He loves it when we come in weakness! So let children *try things* out. I've seen many children exercise spiritual gifts that their parents don't have or use; nevertheless, their parents are delighted for them and are cheering them on.

What has this to do with preparing children for reaching out? For sharing what they believe with others? First, we want them to be excited about God and the incredible things He is doing round the world. I frequently read accounts of or show clips of the miraculous or supernatural from around the world. We witness the crops in Christians' fields growing to enormous size and unaffected by pests and blight! A child is healed of cancer! Let's tell stories and awaken faith and belief in a *big* God.

Our outreach is less about importing models of mission and more about preparing the young to:

a) live with love and compassion for others around them, and

b) move easily in the supernatural so that they have a toolbox of resources at their disposal for their "persons of peace."

Surely this is discipleship for mission. We must not send new young Christians out like lambs to the slaughter, without having had time to learn "how to," practice, or acquire some experience. That would be like me sending my son out for his first bike ride on a road with heavy traffic rather than practicing on quiet paths first!

KEY PRINCIPLE 2: TEACHING AND EXPERIENCING THE SPIRIT'S POWER

Pneumatology (study of the Holy Spirit) has a place in the spiritual formation of the young. We tell the stories of Jesus, but we also need to tell stories about the Person and work of the Holy Spirit. In some countries, boys and girls go to churches where they are taught either nothing, or half-truths, about the Holy Spirit. How can they grow in their faith without knowing *and* experiencing the Holy Spirit? I don't mean to sound flippant, but if I spent seven years being told the same stories again and again, engaging the head without the heart being touched by the *phileo* (demonstrated love of the Father), I'd probably leave too.

I try to ensure that the subject of the Holy Spirit is taught at a cerebral level, welcomed at a personal level, and free at a corporate level, to minister to children.

And as we saw in Key Principle 1, it's through the Holy Spirit that we release our children into the supernatural—there is no junior Holy Spirit! Our faith is not meant to be dull and one-dimensional, but to be felt, experienced, laughed, cried, tried, and practiced. For a child, listening to God is not boring! It's a great thing to be able to pray for others! For more on this topic, read how God uses the young in Iris Ministries' projects in Mozambique.[103] Children have and are daily bringing the Kingdom to earth through the application of their trust in a heavenly Daddy who hears them. I am convinced that all ages modelling this faith to one another will reverse the decline of children from our churches.

Whenever periods of effusion (outpouring of the Holy Spirit) have come upon the church, children have been present. Why? Because children came to meetings with their parents back then? Or is it because they're *not meant to be excluded?* The young Jesus went missing and was found in the temple—is this because being around the place where God's presence is hosted (then it was the temple) is a *natural place for a child to be?* But, you say that the boy Jesus was God's Son, so of course He would have been engaged in worshipful activity. Even so, the mystery of the incarnation is that the boy Jesus was fully human. Can we not expect our children also to have similar feelings? He said to His parents, "Why were you searching for Me? Didn't you know I had to be in My Father's house?"[104] If you have children, you might like to stop for a moment and pray for a hungering after God to increase in them.

Many years ago, I was giving a talk about the Holy Spirit on an Alpha weekend away. I had just prayed and asked the Holy Spirit to come and fill the guests in the room. Some music was playing quietly, and a holy hush seemed to descend on the room. My toddler daughter stopped what she was playing quietly with in the corner and ran to me exclaiming loudly, "Jesus just came in the room! Jesus is here!" Not Jesus in bodily form, but nevertheless, she recognized the presence of God. Everyone heard her say this, and in a moment, the atmosphere was super-charged. Anyone who had doubts before, knew that God was present in a powerful way. Children, because of that "wiring" we discussed in Chapter 1, recognize the presence of God.

Perhaps you are reading this section and wondering how there can be a relationship between children and the Holy Spirit. I have read some books that suggest incredible caution about children and the Holy Spirit. Can or should children be filled with the Holy Spirit? If so, what does it look like? I have already tried to set out the foundations for my belief and practice in Chapters 1 and 2. *It will always come down to these two issues:* Do you believe that children can have a personal faith and love for God and therefore can be filled to overflowing with His Holy Spirit? And do you believe that God is good and that He loves children? He will not lead them into harm. But, of course, we *do* need to be aware of *what* is being taught and *how* it is being taught by adults in positions of trust and responsibility. There is never any need to force an issue.

Remember John Westerhoff's *Theory of Faith Development*? He uses the analogy of a tree to describe the growth of faith in developing human beings. He says, "A tree with one ring is as much a tree as a tree with four rings."[105] In other words, experienced faith, the first stage of faith development, is as valuable for a person to possess as owned faith, the final stage.

So, a child can profess love for God the Father, and Jesus the Son, *and* the Holy Spirit their Helper; but first, children need to be taught about the work and Person of the Holy Spirit. *How can you love someone you hardly know?*

Historical Evidence

Is there any historical evidence of children being filled with the Holy Spirit or exercising spiritual gifts?

Ronald Kydd has examined spiritual gifts in the first three centuries of the Church. He draws a clear conclusion that spiritual gifts were very important in this period, and says:

> We have drawn (material) from virtually every kind of person in the church. We have heard from bishops and heretics,

philosophers and poets, storytellers and theologians. Generally speaking...the church prior to AD 200 was charismatic.[106]

Around AD 177, Bishop Irenaeus provided a list of spiritual gifts seen in Christian communities, and this is very similar to those found in Romans 12 and First Corinthians 12. Irenaeus is just one of a number of Christians from the past who observed gifts in action firsthand and recorded their occurrence for interested parties to read today. Although children are not specifically mentioned, one can assume that children were a part of communal worship. In Chapters 3 and 4, I mentioned that they were learning about faith in action from their parents and the extended community around them. I think we can presume that children were also present when spiritual gifts were being exercised and even practiced them in a very natural way, as part of the Body of believers. Just because we do not specifically read a chapter and verse referencing a child prophesying or exercising the gift of faith, does not mean it did not happen.

There appears to be a dying out of charismatic practices according to written records of early church history after AD 260. Kydd notes that after this point in time, the church was "highly organised, well educated, wealthy and socially powerful,"[107] which sounds remarkably similar to the present day.

Harry Sprange describes many situations from past centuries where children were present during great moves of the Holy Spirit in the nation. Sometimes children were present in the gatherings alongside adults; sometimes there were separate meetings for children. Particularly striking are accounts from the time of George Whitefield's visits to Scotland, from 1741 to 1743, where children under twelve years old heard the preaching to repent and revealed great manifestations of sorrow and subsequent signs of being overcome by the power of the Holy Spirit.

It is difficult when reading snippets of primary sources contained within a secondary source to accurately grasp the extent of how the Scottish revivals affected children. This quote from a Church of Scotland minister, James Robe, in 1734, is a striking example:

> I had a room full of little ones yesternight making a pleasant noise and outcry for Christ; and two of the youngest; one of them but ten years of age, fainting and so distressed they could scarcely go home. I cannot write to you of the wonder I

saw; one of eleven years of age crying out that she was sick of sin, and crying out with hands uplifted to heaven.[108]

The Cane Ridge camp meeting in the state of Kentucky is an example from the United States and of a later date. In 1800, upwards of twelve to twenty-five thousand people of all ages and backgrounds stayed for days and weeks to receive "the mighty power of God…with heavenly fire spreading in all directions."[109] Evidence like this leads to the conclusion that children were not excluded. Whole families came and camped out to partake in the outpouring of the Holy Spirit at that time.

So let us be clear, as with any adult, God wants to fill children with His Holy Spirit and with the overflow of the love *He pours* into their hearts (see Rom. 5:5), they will love and serve other people as Jesus did.

KEY PRINCIPLE 3: SOUND DOCTRINE

We teach children often from a theology built on a narrow collection of Bible stories repeated every two to four years. There is such richness in Scripture, in understanding *who* we are, *what* we've been saved from, and what we've been saved *into*. I concur with George Barna's findings about biblical worldview—erroneous beliefs about Scripture and our key doctrines are creeping up on us. David Kinnaman describes some young people's faith as "inch deep, mile wide";[110] in other words, *shallow*. His research carried out with teen evangelists in 1999 established that very few could identify a single portion of the Bible as the basis of their faith in Christ.[111] Would this be typical amongst the young people you know, work with, or have in your church? It's a question worth reflecting on. The "You Lost Me" research is a gripping read, and I concur wholeheartedly with all of the findings within it.

I also carry a passionate desire to ensure my volunteers have good training and a basic grasp of doctrine and theology. Jesus doesn't physically live inside our hearts, for example; He is now sitting at the right hand of the Father in Heaven!

Some churches, who might hold a different theological perspective from our own, have a lot to offer in this area. Thus, we are being united by a real desire to see children and young people truly grow, experience, and develop as disciples of Jesus in these days. I for one believe good biblical teaching is to accompany the desire to see signs and wonders happen through us.

But how do you know exactly what is being taught to the young in your church? Who decides what's "sound"? How can we make sure the correct truth is being taught?

I have two suggestions to offer in reply to this question:

a. *Stretch and develop your own thinking on how to read the Bible*[112] *or on doctrine.*[113] Don't start with a systematic theology volume, in case it puts you off! Maybe in your denomination or tradition, you use catechisms which would help you decide what is important. If not, ask your pastor(s) and/or check out any denominational guidelines. But don't just stick to what you know; instead, consider reading outside of what you're used to. For example, if you always read Stott, try Wright.[114] One of the greatest lessons I learned from studying for a theology degree was to critically examine why I believed what I believed. This helped me to define what was important to me—and to read and study biblical truth.

As you have probably noticed from earlier chapters, I am not advocating learning catechism by heart, nor am I saying every person who oversees children and family ministry should have a theology degree; but I do wish to highlight that *when we are unsure of what we believe, we may stray into a dilution of doctrinal belief.* I believe it is time to be very intentional in teaching correct biblical doctrines to the young and to those who work with and care for them in any way. I place a high value on equipping and training the teams of volunteers. We (together) want to cultivate deep roots in young believers.

b. *What do you want your own, or other people's, children and teenagers to know, understand, and experience?* Make a list. And use it as something that weaves in and out of everything you do. I don't stand up each week and say to the volunteer teams, "Good morning! This week we are going to make sure we cover the work of the Spirit in reconciliation and adoption!" It's much more subtle than that. My responsibility as a senior staff member is to make sure that over the years we cover these key doctrines and concepts and that they weave in and through what we do.

I deliberately choose (or write) teaching material that covers approximately 80 percent of the subjects listed below. I will supplement other material when I assist existing teams or when I lead response times with the children. I'll cover some of these in certain all-age services or when I meet with the kids' discipleship group. Some of the topics have included:

- Salvation and Assurance

- Sin and Repentance

- Why Did Jesus Die? (the Work of the Cross)

- Jesus' Resurrection and His Place Now in Heaven

- The Trinity

- Jesus—Fully Human and Fully Divine

- Justification

- Reconciliation

- Adoption

- The Person and Work of the Holy Spirit

- Spiritual Gifts

- Satan, God's Enemy

- Jesus' Return and Heaven

Review your own list with your leadership team, explaining the rationale behind your choices, and open up a dialogue as to what you want to ensure children and parents are being taught. My point is that we should have a *plan* of what we want children:

- *to know of God*...through the education and teaching they have received.

- *to live out*...in their personal walk with God day by day, through faithful application of this knowledge, with the gracious help and dynamic empowerment of the Holy Spirit and supported by the faith community.

- *to be able to demonstrate to others, who don't know about the Christian faith (yet),* in a myriad of ways inspired by the Holy Spirit.

Note how these three objectives need to be carried out within a loving, accepting, and nurturing faith community.

If we have no emphasis at all on building community, we may come across as harsh, even legalistic, with a fierce reliance on "right knowledge" and a heavy pressure to evangelize, which may come across as lacking a little in love. On the other hand, too much of an emphasis on *me*, *us*, and *our* community leads to "suffocating" discipleship, elevating love and nurture without biblical regard for the brokenness of our world and its people.

KEY PRINCIPLE 4: WORSHIP AND CHILDREN

What's the worship life of your church's children like? And do they really participate in the worship? If you would observe grown adults, who have just become Christians, looking bored or misbehaving (poking others, for example) during corporate times of worship, you would probably want your leaders to address this type of behavior. I think you'd want the new Christian to see how vital their participation in worship is to their spiritual growth and how it is evidence of a right response to God for all that He has done for us.

Yet often, we don't apply this same thinking or reaction when this scenario involves children. We tolerate disconnection and misbehavior as long as it's quiet and not hurting anyone, because, after all, the children will soon be leaving us for their own groups (or won't be part of the adult service at all). In what ways are we modeling a heart of worship to children? How will children learn about worship? I completely accept that one possible answer is: "It's up to the parents"; but as we know, many parents are looking for support.

Children often can't follow "wordy" songs with many verses on a big screen or in books in a small type-face. They need to move about, and they need to experiment. They benefit from explanations and with descriptive praise (directed toward them). They love to be acknowledged, not because they are hungry for attention, but because it makes them feel valued and loved, welcomed in. They may rarely be referred to in our gatherings—except when they are leaving. The worship leader may reasonably assume that the children are learning how to worship during their separate time away from the adults—except that they might be singing songs that their parents used to sing, with dumbed-down (or plain ludicrous) theology and kindergarten-style actions.

I paint a terribly negative picture, and it may well be a million miles away from your own situation. But I don't think I'm the only one who has heard: "Our worship will begin once the children have left us." So, for some of us, this picture is not too far away from reality. I have visited, taught in, and acted as a consultant for several churches in a number of denominations in the United Kingdom. Many children are not being taught the biblical basis of and for worship, because many of those who lead children lack the knowledge of or the confidence to explain the work of the cross as it pertains to all of our worship. However, *we absolutely must explain the significance of the curtain being torn in two in the temple for all who follow Jesus.* We have free access to the most holy place through the new and living way opened up for us! As for creative ways to retell this story, allow children to experience the "shock and awe" of that day—use pictures, drama, set the scene, build the story, explain the tension, and don't shy away from telling of the supernatural events surrounding the crucifixion, such as the earthquake and the raising of dead people.

I teach children and young people a basic biblical explanation of worship, using Psalm 95, and with an information leaflet to take home and read together as a family about Jesus' death and our journey through praise, worship, adoration, reverence, and intimacy. We want children to learn about the different ways to worship when they are young so that they are more accepting of others and able to be released themselves into different expressions of worship. I have been so pleased as time progresses, to see older children go to the back of the hall to dance with all their might while some of us are standing still, or kneeling, or simply have arms raised—and I know without a doubt that this large number of children under age 12 are worshipping God with *integrity and passion.* For me it's more about that and less about what their limbs are doing. I don't ever want to experience what the Barna Organization found—that in the United States, 69 percent of 13 year olds who profess to be Christians say they have never experienced a sense of God's presence.[115] I find that a disturbing statistic, and again, I can't help but think it must be similar in the United Kingdom in some measure to account for the massive haemorrhage of children outlined in the start of Chapter 6. If we have had a dynamic encounter with God, surely we wouldn't leave Him?

I think the church can sometimes fall into the trap of thinking that if we do some all-age "action" songs that have been used at beach missions, or vacation Bible schools, or summer clubs, then we have met our responsibility and covered what children need from our worship services. *Not so.* They need a living encounter with the manifest presence of God so that they know without a doubt that they have engaged with a powerful God.

Learning and growing in an experience of corporate worship is about real-life intergenerational discipleship. It also leads the young person deeper into the fertile ground that comes from knowing what it is to worship God in the secret place, on your own in your bedroom with your Bible. Recognizing and welcoming the presence of God is an absolute non-negotiable for the "OUT" part of our children and family ministry. Children are simply not going to bring friends to be part of anything that bores them silly. However, they *will* bring them along to something that offers respite from fear, brings joy back to a sad life, comforts lonely hearts, and allows for a lot of active fun!

KEY PRINCIPLE 5: PRAYER AND CHILDREN

Sadly, I've learned that many adults have extremely low expectations of children in the area of prayer. I know God is sovereign and often moves in situations and circumstances despite our weaknesses, but even so, I feel compelled to encourage the youngest ones under my care to think big and talk to God about anything or anyone, anytime and anywhere. He's the One who can do immeasurably more than we ask or imagine (see Eph. 3:20). I read from Scripture that we can come to God expectantly because He is longing to hear our requests.

I recently asked several leaders how children knew that God answered prayer. "Because He does," they replied. I asked them how children would *know* that He does, trying to drive the point home that unless children are hearing the stories of answered prayer, then they are perhaps justified by thinking of Christianity as dull and irrelevant to their fast-moving, social-media dominated world. Children need to see concrete answers to their questions. "Just because He does" holds no power for them. "Prove to me that He does," would be their response. The research accomplished through the "You Lost Me" project provides the evidence: 20 percent of young adults who attended church as a teenager said, *"God seems missing from my experience of church.*"[116] Oh dear Lord, how have we come so far from what You intended the community of faith to be?

This is where parents can be catalysts for change. We saw in Chapter 6 that less than one in ten U.S. Christian families pray or read the Bible together in a typical week.

When I first read these statistics (in 2007), my response was to find out if it was representative of the children and families whom I worked with and for. So I began to ask around in the two large churches I had worked in, and I'd say that for around two hundred children ages five to 11, I witnessed a similar trend. Grace might be said at meals, and Bible stories were occasionally or regularly read; but talking of the things God had done in individual lives, praying together, and giving thanks for answered prayer was definitely not the norm. I began to think, *Why is this?*

Because of the busyness of daily lives, including children's extracurricular activities, whole families sitting down to a meal together is less common, although it is still highly valued in the families I had worked with. This is the time where my own family has a lot of conversation about God, the things He has been doing in our lives, and the answers to prayer that we have seen. When are the times that this can happen otherwise? Bedtime is another good time for this interaction. But I've observed that children are going to bed much later than even twelve years ago when my daughter was a baby. Some children get themselves off to bed with no adult intervention; and others go harassed by a parent who doesn't have time for extended Bible or prayer time. The ever-present gadgets and visual stimuli in our homes are undoubtedly stealing away time from families to talk and pray together. Long working hours for one or both parents and the pressure to maintain an active, balanced life means less time is given over to simply "being" as a family, at home together.

This picture of increasingly separate, partitioned off-blocks of time is alien to families in many cultures who live, work, and play together in challenging circumstances in less developed parts of our world. We need to be intentional about carving out precious family time if we are to ground our children in whole-life discipleship that helps us to identify and pray for the ones God is leading us to—the persons of peace introduced at the start of this chapter. I am convinced the pressures and busyness of life are the enemy's chief strategies to prevent a movement toward household reorientation in significant numbers. I've witnessed children (not teenagers!) with five or six extra-curricular commitments after school and on weekends, working parents, and lots of homework. Finding time for family prayer and individual devotions is not impossible, but is certainly most difficult.

Many other parents have confessed to me that they struggle with praying with their children and have become stuck in a pattern, which quite frankly is boring them (and possibly their child). Their child doesn't seem to want to pray with them, and both parties just want to get it over with as quickly as possible.

I want to briefly outline some ways to reawaken your church's, family's, or children's prayer life. I hope you can see too that what I write below is for *the whole family* who may come brand-new to the Christian faith. This is not all about children—many adults get stuck in their own prayer life as well.

Reawakening and Refreshing Prayer in Children and Families

a. Moving Children on in Prayer

Steps 1 to 5 are suggestions by John and Chris Leach.[117]

> Step 1—leader/parent does everything—chooses a prayer subject, prays about it, and says "amen" at the end. Subjects need to be simple and relevant, linked to the everyday life or the Bible story you may have just read. The leader/parent models short prayers. Eventually the children join in with "amen."

> Step 2—the children repeat prayers phrase by phrase with their leader/parent.

> Step 3—the children are asked to suggest items for prayer, then back to step 2.

> Step 4—children suggest items for prayer and the leader/parent suggests how they might pray. This could be a set formula like "Dear Lord, please look after _____ this week. Amen."

> Step 5—Children think of an issue and pray out loud.

What follows is my own suggestion:

> Step 6—children lay hands on one another and pray simple prayers for the leader and for one another; they are able to deliver words and pictures, and ask God to intervene in situations. Their boldness grows the more they practice. This step requires children to be taught that God speaks as we listen. The Alpha course manual (Week 6) includes a helpful list of the different ways in which God speaks and guides; this manual can be used with children and young people fairly regularly.

Step 6 is ideally practiced in a variety of settings, such as Sunday gatherings, midweek intergenerational house groups, missional communities (see next chapter), or in a public outreach.

Use descriptive praise toward the children to mark the movement from one stage to another. Consider using a prayer journal to record answers to prayer. Faith is built when we receive answers and we celebrate each little success, which creates a desire to pray more and causes higher levels of expectation.

b. 24/7 Prayer Rooms

When my church entered wholeheartedly into regular 24-hour seasons of prayer, seven days a week (in a dedicated room in the church building), I couldn't help but immediately think, *Why can't children and families visit this together?* So I set about encouraging whole families to do this. I wrote to parents before the prayer room week began, enclosing a leaflet with some information on how children engage with God and some practical suggestions on how to spend a one-hour time slot in the prayer room with young children.

The prayer room had a chalkboard wall where people could write verses and draw pictures, with pegs and hanging space, post-it notes, paper, and pens. It was warmly furnished with cushions and blankets. I placed a box marked "children's resources" with sponges, paints, rollers, sugar paper, and crayons, as well as a selection of age-appropriate Bibles. This was a great success and used by many families who might not have gone all together to pray. Several families with older teenagers also went together. They usually sat in different places in worship services, but they went to the prayer room together!

Children, some very young, listened to God, prayed for the church and the nation, and received prophetic words and pictures, which were displayed on the "community wall." Immediately they felt part of the church's prayer life. I relayed these examples (showing photographs, etc.) in services, and some of the children themselves shared their own story of how they found the prayer room to be a place where they met with God. I have to say that the family stories have greatly touched me, and I have been genuinely privileged to watch this blessing unfold. And this is not difficult for readers to imagine happening in your own place! Inspiring stories and lots of help on how to start a prayer room is available online.[118]

This room played a part, I believe, in catapulting our church children forward in their expectation of and journey with prayer.

c. Church Prayer Meetings

It was a short step for me to proceed in arranging for time in our regular prayer meetings to be given over to all ages coming together to worship and pray, to tune in to God, and to pray for the church, the city, and the nation. We also enjoyed gentle but powerful times of children praying for—really ministering the power of the Holy Spirit—to adults and adults praying for children. On one occasion, I had put together a "tabernacling space," where a young boy who very rarely came to church was lying down in God's presence. Watching my senior pastor gently pray for him, and minister something from God Himself to this young boy's hurting spirit was like watching a little bit of Heaven unfold before me. I'll never forget what I saw happening in the spirit. Imagine making time for such encounters in God's presence between adults and children in your faith community.

Why not make your church prayer meetings accessible to all ages for the first hour? Make sure it's not dry and boring. Try to use a gifted worship leader or prayer leader who can engage all ages together. It's not an easy thing to do; we have had to start our prayer meetings earlier and stay longer ourselves after the children and families have gone home, but it is a cost I gladly pay. Imagine the new families who are to come into the Kingdom joining in with these kinds of activities! They will grow in faith and in experiences. Don't worry if you are not sure how the event will turn out. The one lesson I have learned most over the years through making mistakes is that God honors the heart behind what we do. It's as if He is particularly inclined toward our attempts to see children grow in experience of Him and in prayer.

d. Children Praying for Others

I want to stress that the journey I have outlined above from traditional Sunday school to 24/7 prayer room to church prayer meetings to ministering to one another and praying for schools and families, for the sick and the hurting, happened very quickly (in 12 to 18 months); and therefore, I believe the same is eminently possible for any church that takes seriously the call to nurture and disciple the young to take great strides forward. I simply facilitated and then stepped back.

I began to see a change by disseminating everything I knew and practiced about children's innate spirituality to parents and the wider church by any means possible (annual Vision days, meetings with key individuals, all-age services, "family slots," emails, pastoral home visits, written reports). I wanted to raise the expectation levels by explaining and demonstrating that children connect with God easily and believe for big things. I then planned to take children on from wherever they were in prayer using the six steps previously listed. All along, I encouraged children and leaders to listen carefully as to how they should pray because we have an *almighty* powerful God who is longing to move in response to our prayers. Therefore, in the first year, I spent quite a lot of time teaching my volunteer team and the children themselves to listen out for God and not to dive in, praying what *they* thought was best without asking God for direction as to how they should pray.

I also led a group of children who were hungry, very hungry to know God more, and we worked through the Power of the Praying Kid[119] book. This was no ordinary discipleship group; we met every third week, and in between those times, I authored a history-maker sheet to be given to a parent, summarizing what we had done and setting some homework (!) for the parent and child to do together. For example, one of the instructions included: "Tell your child about a time you had to forgive someone. Was this easy or hard? What happened once you had done that? What did it feel like?"

So, children practiced the laying on of hands, and waiting on God, listening to Him first for Bible verses or pictures before praying for an adult's need (visas, accommodation, final exams). This was a weekly occurrence. Rather than leading this from the front, I introduced the activity and let the children gather round individuals and pray. Sometimes my team and I wanted to conclude the praying time so that we could move on to another programmed activity, but there would be very few children sitting on the floor waiting. They were usually crowded around a person or persons being prayed for, laying hands on and watching, listening, and joining in. I learned to just go with this. *There is a rising hunger amongst children to pray—and I would urge you not to hold this back. Go with it.*

It's very important to share the answers to prayer so that children match up the beginning with the end and realize that God always answers prayer. This also allows them to see that sometimes the answer is "no" or "wait." And it allows them to grow in bold faith.

One week, a nurse who was off work with a slipped disc came into the children's hall to seek prayer specifically because she had heard that the children offered to pray for people. A crowd of about thirty children dutifully laid hands on her and prayed with faith for her back—very simply, but boldly. She had an appointment later that week with the occupational health specialist who had signed her off work. At that appointment, the specialist substantiated that the nurse had been healed of all pain and the disc was back in place, so she could return to work.

After hearing the report, I asked her to come back to tell the children exactly what had happened in the previous seven days. Naturally, their faith was strengthened because they had experienced God's power working through them, which I reckon they will never forget.

The journey from a traditional classroom-based Sunday school to what I have described above (in two years) continues, as children now pray in school for their friends to be healed of headaches and stomach upsets. Friends, this journey is not an impossibly hard one. God is committed where you feel weak because (I am convinced) He loves to hear children praying.

And I've witnessed children taking their experiences of prayer from the classroom with their friends to their families, leading them forward in their experiences of God. Earlier, I wrote of the example in China— could we even be seeing the signs of a missional movement emanating from children to parents right now—*here* in our Western churches?

The journey in and with prayer for children is an essential one, I believe, so that we can be ready for what is to come. New Christians, with no relatives who have gone before them to help show them the way, will need to be in direct and continual dialogue with their Father in Heaven. They'll need—and I believe will receive—bold and radical answers to prayer that will see a reorientation throughout their extended family toward God and lifelong commitments to the Christian faith.

KEY PRINCIPLE 6: MISSION AND CHILDREN

It is imperative that we challenge and encourage children to think about and to live out a missional life—desiring to make disciples of those who don't yet know Jesus. This sixth principle supports almost all other work of training and equipping children, described in the other five key principles.

- We need to ensure children have a *knowledge and experience of God* so that they demonstrate it (not just tell it) to those who most need to know. So, for example, I found myself being asked by another parent why my own son seemed to have an ability to be very gentle and compassionate (their words), while still being a rough-and-tumble soccer-loving boy. What a privilege to be able to talk about the difference living for Jesus has made to him!

- Children have a personal encounter with the *Spirit's power* so that they are sent out with boldness and courage as their standard, and not timidity and fear.

- We ensure a deep *knowledge and appreciation of the key truths in Scripture* so that what is communicated and passed on to others outside of our church world is truth. We want to grow other disciples from the scattering of good seed.

- We *worship* so that we receive a fresh revelation of the majesty and supremacy of God who cares for us deeply, tenderly, and intimately. As a husband and wife team who lead worship and believe and practice all that we have written in this book, we know this to be central in our own missional activity. Face-to-face worship encounters can't help but transform us, and in my experience, actually draw others to Christ in us! Matt Redman wrote,

"Let worship be the fuel for mission's flame,"[120] and I passion-ately agree. Let us see this in the young and for the young.

- *Prayer* is the lifeline that connects our young missional disciples with the Father who sends them out and who cares deeply for their own needs and well-being. When we engage in prayer for those outside our faith community, we pick up on God's com-passionate, loving heart for the broken and the lost. We should give children appropriate experiences that allow their hearts to be softened toward other people and their situations.

When we "tell" people (of any age) to "do" mission, the ensuing guilt may weigh them down so that they labor from a place of "ought to" rather than "want to." A life lived in submission to God and to others and marked by joy and intimacy leads us out. I pray that this lifestyle is modeled by others—primarily by parents as they spend the most time and exert the most influence over their offspring—and also by others in the faith community who play a major part in showing how it can be.

Chapter Eight

DRAWING IT ALL TOGETHER

In the last chapter, I introduced some key principles on which to build children and family ministry. You will have noted that I didn't particularly restrict what I wrote to children only or to adults only—the point being that I cannot separate out what I have experienced into neat little boxes. These key principles apply to both children and adults. In review, these key principles include:

1. Knowledge and experience.

2. Teaching and experiencing the Holy Spirit's power.

3. Sound doctrine.

4. Worship and children (applies to adults as well).

5. Prayer and children (applies to adults as well).

6. Mission and children (applies to adults as well).

THE WIND OF THE SPIRIT

In my ministry to date, I've looked for flexible models of inclusivity, discipleship, and mission that include families and that which looks more like Old and New Testament community. In this chapter, I want to outline some events, structures, or ways of working that make room for the six key principles above. Please note that you and I can pick up *ideas* from events, structures, and ways of working without importing them whole scale. We can be influenced without copying every detail because we each have our own context that becomes a vehicle for modification and interpretation. And this, I believe, is where we need the wind of the Holy Spirit—allow Him to sweep over all your plans, thoughts, and ideas. In Acts chapter 2, when the Holy Spirit came in power on the followers of Jesus, the result was that they were sent out into the city, the region, the nation, and the world.

Here is a very personal example, which occurred in 2006. My first two years as a children's and family pastor were spent getting to know children and their families and setting up good administration systems, training volunteers, putting together sound teaching, blending with the rest of the staff team, and playing my part in gathered worship services. After two years, I was ready for the next level.

I attended a conference in March 2006 entitled, "Families on Fire" at Toronto Airport Christian Fellowship[121] and witnessed the high value placed on children and family ministry, not just by the children's pastors Daphne and Darrin Clark, but by the whole church. I took my six-year old daughter with me, and we watched how all the children present listened to the teaching (soundly biblical, open to the Holy Spirit, not dumbed-down, yet all-age appropriate) and how they responded to God at the conference. I was encouraged and challenged by what I saw; it made me think that this must have been what had happened in the first century. Children, as individuals, and their whole families, owned the church's vision statement: "to walk in God's love and give it away, until the whole earth is filled with the knowledge of the glory of the Lord."[122] My observation was that children were activated as natural missionaries in and through all that the children's ministry department does there.

I could have come back and gone straight into organizing something similar, but I didn't. I waited and took six months to reflect and process before talking my ideas over with my trusted senior pastor. As a result, in October 2007, I conducted a "Families on Fire" conference for *all ages together* in Scotland. Over 250 people attended. We taught on who we are in Christ, what we have been called to do in following Jesus, how to honor one another within our families, and the importance of forgiveness. We taught everyone how to listen to God. We spent a couple of hours soaking[123]—being still—in God's presence. The children who had never experienced this before took to it, like ducks to water. This was the first conference that I know of in the United Kingdom for all ages together. I still cherish the memory of three generations of one family praying with one another regarding all that was ahead for them as grand-parents, children, and grandchildren.

The feedback to the conference was remarkably positive, sending the overwhelming message that many families had for the first time encountered God together and found it life-changing. For sure, it was not difficult to make happen, mainly because of the fantastic support which my senior pastor, the elders, and the administrative staff gave to me. They also believed in the vision and purpose of the conference. In addition, I had a context that allowed this to happen. You may not have been blessed with those circumstances—yet. Often we push for an outcome to happen because we think it *should* happen. Indeed, I am so grateful for the teams with whom I have been privileged to work. (In Chapter 9, we will look at the importance of "team.")

So, 2006-07 marked a gear change for me when I saw remarkable blessings take place in children's ministry in tandem with "adult" ministry. I have received positive feedback *whenever* I have simply planned times for adults and children to be together in worship, prayer, or to receive teaching from the Bible. To see tears fall from a dad's face as his children gently pray for him, to watch children pray for leaders and vice versa, to see a recently widowed young mother cuddle up close to her children as other people minister so gently to them as a family unit. These are the results I count as a huge privilege to have witnessed. Your church can too.

As I have addressed in previous chapters of this book, we desperately need something to change in the relatively wealthy Western Church. We seem to be in a time where new wineskins are needed, when what we have always done is so clearly not working like it should. I am not alone in feeling this way; over the past decade or so, there has been a growing dissatisfaction in many denominations and places of the world with our experience of "church." I think this has come out of a shift in considering how we reach out. There is a lot of talk on how to be more missional. Has the Western Church realized that she is no longer in a period of *evangelization*, but a period of *mission?* This understanding, therefore, requires less of a reactive knee-jerk response, as in "We need to be doing..." and more of a fundamental reorientation of *why* we meet together. I read recently:

> A mission field requires a different approach. Instead of evangelisation campaigns designed to get the lapsed back into

church, the challenge is much more long-term and incarnational—to take the gospel to the people around us in their di-
verse cultures and help them to become disciples of Jesus
Christ within those cultures. Instead of trying to get new believers from a very different culture to fit into the inherited culture of our existing cultures, the challenge is to build church
around those new believers within their own culture. This requires new forms of church for a new missionary situation.[124]

These words highlight the reason for this book. We cannot simply
evangelize the millions of children, those who are most open to the incredible Good News that we carry, those who so easily grasp Kingdom principles with teachable spirits and open hearts, who will naturally and easily
tell others about the greatness of God, *without changing what we do.*

Readers, it is time to end the continual partitioning or excluding of
children from key events in the life of the church. I pray that we would
live out the words: "You are welcome here. You have things to teach us.
You have a heart that captures the very essence of the Kingdom." It is
never under debate that we have much knowledge and understanding to
impart to children. That fact that children need us for their physical and
spiritual growth and care has never been disputed. But the fact that we
might *need* children can be an uncomfortable one as it challenges our
structures and even our very own sense of self-worth and identity. Many
of us don't like the idea that young ones may have something to teach us.
We are so used to children and young people fitting into plans that we
have already made.

I do want to make it clear that our disregard of children is often unintentional; we often become so swept along with the plans for the new
building, the new vision, or the new leaders, that we often overlook the
ones not yet the same height as us. If you are in a position where you
make decisions regarding the operation and spiritual oversight of a
church, take time to listen to those who speak for the younger generations. If your children's ministry leaders ask questions about your future
plans, it's not to be awkward or disloyal, it's because they might see opportunities or challenges that you have not been aware of.

We can't afford to ignore the spiritual growth and development of the
young for we *need* them. Who on your leadership team advocates for
them? Remember too that *if* children are indeed significant in the coming

revival, *if* God wants to restore healthy relationships to families so that they can see transformation, then there is an enemy who wants to sow mistrust, suspicion, and dissension. Let's determine together to disciple and nurture the youngest as well as the most vocal, the weakest who have so little as well as the most influential who give time and money, the ones who are satisfied with being loved and not constantly complaining at what is happening in "their" church.

MAKING SPACE FOR MINISTRY TO AND WITH ENTIRE FAMILIES

What follows are descriptions of a few programs that may spark ideas for you and your church. I include a lengthier section on missional communities because this topic is one that many people are beginning to hear about. These type of communities are springboards to the kind of change in direction and focus that many of our churches need if we are to move forward in these years of long-term incarnational mission to households around us. Read with excitement and faith, remembering what we reviewed about New Testament times (Chapter 4)—that the church grew as whole households with people of all ages and stages of life reoriented themselves to Jesus and established relational networks. Read this chapter also keeping in mind that we are now looking at ways of working that are orientated firmly OUTward (review Chapter 6), ways that will equip every one of us with regard to our connections outside the church. This is missional discipleship.

These programs include:

1. Sunday @ 5

2. Kings Kids International (YWAM)

3. Teatime Alpha

4. Missional Communities

SUNDAY @ 5

Sunday @ 5 is an intergenerational, inter-church gathering which meets weekly in a housing estate in Barton, Oxford. Its roots began with an action group who met to pray and dream of how to make connections with the residents of Barton.

After hosting a "Christmas Churches Together" event and an "Easter Fun-day," a steering group met for discussion and realized that it wasn't easy to invite people to activities inside the church. Thus came the question: what form should future gatherings take? The group developed a questionnaire asking: "If Carlsberg did church, what would it look like?" and took this form door-to-door to ask those neighbors what they should include. From here, came an invite to the first Sunday @ 5—with a free BBQ and games.

The service has continued and includes four elements: (a) welcome; (b) sharing food; (c) activities, games, and crafts; and (d) teaching, prayer, and worship.

After the welcome, the other elements vary in length and order. The most common pattern is welcome, song, a brief all-age talk, prayer time, activities, and food. In so doing, this gathering provides an opportunity for adults and children to be together in an open and honest setting. Feedback to prayer is given, and the community has seen some healing miracles.

What draws these people to come to the gatherings? It seems to be a combination of answers. First, it involves Christians building relationships with people outside of the church and then inviting them to activities. For others, it's the sense of welcome and belonging, alongside receiving acts of kindness during the week. The program is constructed to include people of all ages who don't have a long history of church attending. There is less singing, simple lyrics, direct "all-age style" talks, and a sense of "being real" with prayer requests.

Sunday @ 5 is a place for people at all stages of faith development. It provides warmth, love, and acceptance. It provides a place for those who want to belong, makes space for those who have hard questions to ask or who just want to watch, *and* a place for those at the "owned faith" stage.

While talking with someone who has been involved with this project, I learned that they attribute the program's success to the fact that people who would not otherwise go to Sunday morning church feel part of a community of believers.

KING'S KIDS INTERNATIONAL

King's Kids International (KKI) is a worldwide movement, part of YWAM (Youth With A Mission), and for over 35 years has modelled ways of reaching, discipling, and mobilizing all ages together. It asks each of the generations to honor one another and to cooperate in order to see God move.[125]

Intergenerational ministry and service teams are now commonplace in approximately one hundred nations, as very young children, pre-teens, youth, and adults all join together to know God more and make Him known. In deciding to provide activities for whole families, KKI encourages a lifestyle where worship, listening to God's voice, and a missionary vision are incorporated into the daily life of a family. This provides an opportunity for families to be active in discipling their children into a lifestyle of mission and to gather together in larger groups to do so, once more reinforcing the opportunities for family, clan, and tribe to serve God faithfully as one unit.

In the United Kingdom, KKI operates as *Wildfire*, to partner with families and youth in local churches, sharing and imparting ways to start being truly intergenerational.

My friends, Andy and Catherine Kennedy, currently lead this ministry in the United Kingdom and have seen family mission teams sent out to over fifty nations in the last twenty years. They stress that any Christian community can partner with KKI to release families with children of all ages into creative ways of doing mission. I would add that underpinning everything in YWAM is the need for "heart prep"—being in right relationship with God and removing anything that impinges on this goal. Being part of a KKI team is beneficial to the individual, the family, the local church to which the family belongs, *and* the community they go to serve on their short-term local outreach.

TEATIME ALPHA

Simply, this program is conducting an Alpha course at a time that suits the families involved. In my first church, I had asked people, who included those who parented alone, or who didn't have babysitters on hand, to come to an event one evening. I wondered if I could create community by providing a lovely meal and a warm welcome beginning at 6:00 P.M., which the whole family could attend.

Starting in 2006, once a year, for eleven Friday nights,[126] entire families have attended, and I could not have guessed how naturally this program would develop. Dads rush in from work to sit with their partners, knowing that dinner will be served; children are served by caring volunteers; dishes are washed afterward by the Alpha Team— and the result is that the guests are relaxed, open, and ready for great discussion times. The whole evening does not last more than one hour 45 minutes by using the Alpha Express DVDs.[127]

For the first hour, we all are together chatting and eating, and for 45 minutes the children are cared for by a team of volunteers who do some crafts with them in a way that allows for very natural and gentle opportunities to talk about God. On the Holy Spirit week (the one week that does last longer than the regular time), the children join their parents, and my team and I ask permission to pray for the whole family. Consent has always been given, and so, in a very moving experience, we lay hands on the family and ask God to bless them. It's often at this time that we have specific words of knowledge for individual children, and with permission, we share these words where appropriate. We also show the parents how to pray for their child(ren). (I'm always keen to teach on the power of blessing.)

We then pray for adults and children together at the end of each evening, which gently introduces a habit that parents might continue, whether or not they transition to church (although our earnest desire is that they will). A few of the families who have attended Alpha later found a real home in the intergenerational house groups (see Chapter 6), which I had set up initially, almost as an experiment, as a way of dealing with my frustration that no programs were being offered before 7:30 P.M. These groups are still going strong four years later (and I have nothing to do with them, as I have moved to another job!), and they bear the most resemblance to the supportive group that formed during Teatime Alpha.

I write about this early evening Alpha course at this point of the book because I want to illustrate that once again the aim is to create community, create a setting that not-yet-churched people want to come to because they experience acceptance and love toward their *whole* family. With Alpha, the pressure is off to succeed—all we have to do is completely and genuinely care for the families. We don't have to force or manipulate a certain outcome, because it is the Holy Spirit's role to work in the lives of the individuals we meet. What I love most is that creating community is the easiest thing in the world to do. You simply begin with making an opportunity for it to happen, and then stand back and watch what forms naturally. Older children get drinks for younger children, adults chat to children who aren't their own flesh and blood, wee ones look up to the role modelling of those older than them, frazzled moms begin to relax, and so on.

Obviously, this course is just that—a course; so it does not incorporate all six of the key principles listed at the start of this chapter and introduced in the previous chapter—children don't learn how to worship, for example. Nevertheless, as I reflect on my "learning on the job" journey with Teatime Alpha, I saw a fresh desire awaken in the "churched" children to think of friends' families they could invite along and watched them as they passionately did all they could to make this happen.

MISSIONAL COMMUNITIES

What place do missional communities have in allowing children intentional opportunities to act on their faith? And what makes this different from a "standard church service"?

Many churches in the United Kingdom are the size of a mid-sized group—a missional community of twenty to fifty people who gather together. There are several reasons why I think these communities are ideal gatherings in which to base many of the events or strategies I have outlined thus far.

Previously, I had laid out the evidence that something is *not* working with regard to standard worship services, as we witness many congregations that are aging rapidly and where the attendance of children continues to decrease. Moreover, I feel that many of our structures and traditions are stifling *something* that is struggling to be birthed. I simply appeal to you to read on to see if there is any idea that could be applied to your situation.

I want to address the topic of missional communities because I discern there is a prophetic restlessness in the church just now. It seems to be that we are waiting for something—not "the next big thing" or some kind of trend—but something that will indeed allow many people to access Jesus and help herald His return. I believe missional communities bring us closer to what is described in the Old and New Testaments than anything else I have seen or experienced. What I write now is not an either/or for your situation, but to be pondered and prayed through and perhaps even experimented with. To this end, there are publications and support structures that can offer far more information and advice on this subject than I can here,[128] but I do want to bring some theological and practical reflection arising out of my own experiences with missional communities and from a case study at St Thomas Philadelphia, Sheffield (England).[129]

Teaching children and families, who are new to the faith, about the need to be missional, comes from the idea of discipleship, which follows becoming part of the family of God. It is a fundamental part of a child's training and is actually *much easier* instilled at the very *beginning* of a person's faith journey. It's harder to persuade people who are quite comfortable with a cozy church experience!

There are many debates about what comes first—mission or discipleship, and I have observed what happens when one camp feels the other camp has neglected their cause. But of one fact I am certain—we need to know *who we are* in Christ, *what we are equipped with*, and *in whose Name and power we go*; or else we who pastor will end up with needless casualties of war.

In 2011, I followed a wide-ranging debate on this issue on Mike Breen's blog.[130] Mike recommends the use of huddles (a discipleship and leadership vehicle) and missional communities (a discipleship and mission vehicle) *at the same time*, to recreate communities more like the New Testament model of church. As he says so simply: "If you make disciples well, like Jesus did, you will get the missional thing."

We're often polarized into churches who are strong on pastoral care and nurture (IN), or churches that are passionately missional (OUT); and if we manage to combine IN and OUT together, it's often at times that don't suit children or families (evenings after 7:30 P.M.). In the realm of kids' work, there may be a noticeable imbalance—lots of nurture and care and less outreach. Or we hold a big summer mission to reach children, yet neglect to provide for them in ways that cater for their needs in our worship services for the other eleven months and three weeks of the year. I am deeply concerned by the lack of emphasis on a three-dimensional lifestyle for children.

I remember speaking in a faltering voice at a session of the Families on Fire conference mentioned earlier (in 2007) to all ages together. I specifically spoke about rediscovering what it would look like to impact those who don't know Jesus by being missional in community *together, all the time, as a lifestyle choice.* I had begun my journey that brings me to this point, and I am sure there is more to discover and learn from others on the journey ahead!

So, missional communities involve discipleship and mission together. For example, my family and I were part of a missional community which had a heart to support and influence the local primary school. One of the members led a Scripture Union (SU) group at the school and then gave regular updates about the group; in addition, the volunteers and the children who attended SU were regularly prayed for by our missional community. This is an example of a local church supporting the work of the Scripture Union group in a way that was close to their heart and vision as a group.

What is a missional community?

Very simply, a missional community (MC) is an outward-focused group of people. The formal (and very helpful) definition from the field guide regarding the setting up of missional communities describes them as:

> Groups of anything from twenty to no more than fifty people who are united, through Christian community, around a common service and witness to a particular neighbourhood or network of relationships. With a strong value on life together, the group has the expressed intention of seeing those the group impacts start following Jesus, through this more flexible and locally incarnated expression of the church.[131]

They meet as part of the gathered church some of the time and meet as a separate community at other times. They are led by lay leaders. In some larger churches who already operate MCs, the central ministry staff empower and equip the missional community leaders. I would say that as a church grows, this support becomes essential as missional communities will need help in specialist areas, such as safeguarding vulnerable adults or supporting people with addictions. The focus is decided by the embryonic missional community members, rather than prescribed by staff.

The idea is that MCs grow and replicate themselves through the process of belonging and believing—and this expected growth illustrates the very foundation of missional communities. We know that people are more likely to be receptive to faith when it is demonstrated to them by people within their own network of friendships and relationships.[132]

In my home nation of Scotland, many churches are in reality the size of missional communities (20 to 50 people), and I hope that what follows on modeling and encouraging missional discipleship in mid-sized communities will be helpful.

When do missional communities meet, and what do they do?

The guiding principle here is "high accountability, low control." MC leaders meet with other leaders and staff members for training and resourcing, but they are free, within limits, to decide much for themselves. The meeting time and place is defined by the missional context and the community, not the church calendar or past history or traditions. It is a lighter, more flexible way of being church that caters to the needs of the community, which is exactly why I think all of us involved in ministry should consider implementing such a program. I have found that my experiences within these communities have caused me to rethink much of what I do and why I do it.

So, is the responsibility of a missional community to do mission or grow disciples? Some say it's mission. Some say it's discipleship. Some say it's both. My personal belief is that we need to support sending each other out after we have been immersed in a context of nurture and discipleship, especially so with our youngest members of the faith community, in order that we protect them from all that is raging against them. I think there is no doubt that young Christ-followers are immediately submersed in a counter-culture the minute they leave our company to go to school. Mike Breen and Steve Cockram write: "If you set out to make disciples, you will inevitably build the church."[133]

Throughout this book I have been encouraging you to think of how you can play a part in discipling children. If fifty or a hundred children with no prior church background showed up on a Sunday, what would you do with them? What would you teach them? How would you integrate them into the life of the church more fully? How would you ensure that their embryonic faith survives in an increasingly antagonistic culture? *I'm suggesting that one of the ideal God-ordained places to raise* children as *"missional disciples"* is in a missional community. This mid-sized group will also have scope to run two or more smaller groups offering pastoral care and discipleship.

Serving Children in Missional Communities

I have two observations to make:

(a) From the outset, consider how you will ensure each (relevant) MC accomplishes your church's vision or ethos for children and teenagers. Is there a *holistic approach* to see children as part of a family? After all, this is how statutory agencies see children. For example, the last thing you want an MC to do is to reach adults yet neglect or ignore the needs of children. Or for the MC to better the lives of children in desperate poverty but never consider how to minister to the family of those children.

Also, your church's core values (the DNA) need to be sharp, clear, and communicated to each MC so that they can replicate this DNA in all that they do. As I have stated before, you should be well informed about your church's views, beliefs, and vision for children and young people. If you're not aware of these, your MCs may evolve to see children and teenagers with many different theologies and views on what's best for them. I would strongly urge you to work this through together and write a vision statement. Chapter 9 will provide some pointers to accomplish this task.

Assuming you already have a vision statement for your children's and family ministry, how can you transfer the nuts and bolts of this objective to the MC leaders? And where can you apply some flexibility so that MC leaders can develop their own response to the growth that comes their way? If you can provide for this to happen, there will be a glorious freedom when the groundwork has been prepared. Whereas, if there is no input from your leaders, will the MC leaders know and understanding your church's view of children? This question is not about control; it's about making sure we have a rock-steady foundation for the growth in ministry that *will* come. God is preparing us for a flood of children to come into a vibrant, lifelong relationship with Jesus.

Leaving these questions unanswered until after multiple MCs have been launched is too late, and we lose something of the importance of children and family ministry as it then becomes an extra responsibility that hard-pressed, busy people find extremely difficult to take on. Thus, your church's high-level vision and appropriate teaching to adults (see Chapter 6) are essential because they ensure that young people have their rightful place as new initiatives begin.

(b) Regarding what children learn and experience when they are participate in the MCs, how will you ensure that what you do in the center dovetails with this and vice versa? Children learn by building, or "scaffolding," meaning that a new piece of knowledge or experience is tacked on to something they already know or have done; so, the last thing we want to do is have children go back and forth each week, jumping from one topic to the next, in their learning and experience. For example, consider the following proposed schedule for an MC:

> Week 1—participate in the Central gathering—Sunday school—Noah's ark.

> Week 2—at the MC, look at how we can control our thought life with the Spirit's help.

> Week 3—craft Sunday—build straw puppets to act out the story of David and Goliath.

> Week 4—MC—worship and testimony meeting; halfway through this time, children leave the room for a snack break and to watch a DVD.

This outline may seem like a haphazard list, but is it really so far from reality? I suggest not. Each one of these weeks of teaching has its own merit, with a lot of helpful Scripture applications; but is it possible that the see-saw nature of the experience means that very little learning roots in deeply? Where, for adults, we often teach a "series" or recap last week's small group time with questions such as, "How did you apply what you learned last week?" which allows for repetition and to build upon the previous week's learning.

Let's not shortchange children by disregarding what is best for them. We realize that church isn't school, so we don't want to follow an inflexible and highly structured schedule, but sadly we often swing between two extremes—regimented classroom or a random "whatever fits with us as adults."

Consider early on how you will provide teaching input to children and teenagers. Make it a priority and designate substantial time and effort at the center to develop a teaching plan for the whole church. Then release key staff members to work alongside the leadership team to look at specific areas of focus you might have during certain months (e.g., outreach to children and families during the summer), so that resourcing is applied appropriately. During Advent I would, for example, envision writing the following outline:

> Week 1—Central gathering—"the Light has come"—practical ways of bringing light to our communities through our MCs (vision casting!)
>
> Week 2—MC—Jesus fully human and fully divine (teach this at the center also for MCs who are "in" that week)
>
> Week 3—Christmas story—Bible passage
>
> Week 4—MC—the reality of the promise that God is with us, as this affects our everyday lives and the challenges we are struggling with.

It has probably become apparent that this endeavor will take some planning, but it's not impossible. There are churches who have planned in a similar style. But remember, it is not critical that MCs follow the same weekly theme as the central worship service nor even as each other. I use the above suggestion only to illustrate that for consistency and growth in our children and young people, we need to think "build, build, build." This does not need mean that we must concentrate on the Book of Romans for fifty-two consecutive weeks! However, bearing in mind the Barna research regarding the lack of a biblical worldview in U.S. churches (see Chapter 6), we may want to take a closer look at what we do teach.

A Case Study—St Thomas Philadelphia, Sheffield

At the time of this writing, there are approximately 120 missional communities at St Thomas Philadelphia, Sheffield. About 40 to 45 of these communities are for youth, children, and families. Some of these are youth only, but many are generationally mixed. Each MC chooses how they will operate (all ages together, children separated all of the time, or part of each), and all the MCs hold social events where everyone mixes together. Likewise, they all maintain a three-fold emphasis on UP-IN-OUT.

At the MC level, the children's ministry staff and/or leaders empower and resource the MC leader to lead the children in their community (activity/craft/teaching/games, etc.), which means the staff may help for a season at the start and provide resources. Children's material is available; nevertheless, it is up to the MC leader to choose a series. This means the teaching is not the same across all the MCs: some take the material and use it to the letter; others accept it as a guide and adapt or mesh it with other teaching.

At the cell level (called "God's Gang"), a children's leader leads the group with at least one parent, with the aim that in time the parents themselves will lead. This provides support to the parent but breaks the "provider-client" dynamic that can occur when the assumption is that the expert will look after or disciple the children. Each week, there is provision for the children at the central campus for those MCs who are not meeting on their own that week, and in case of visitors or new people who have not settled in to MCs yet.

Every MC attends the Sunday gathering on the first of each month and meets somewhere outside the center on the last Sunday of the month. During the intervening two Sundays, the MCs decide when and where they will meet.

The entire senior leadership team of St Thomas Philadelphia hold a high view of children and young people. They have had a long time (15 years or more) to build a model, which allows for coherence and consistency in the teaching and experiences for children and young people. They have also been careful to retain significant central functions, such as child protection training and internal learning communities at which MC leaders attend for envisioning and forward planning. In the children and family ministry—worship celebrations, evangelistic events, and a leadership training school for children themselves are some of the central functions.

AN IDEAL PLACE FOR CHILDREN
AND FAMILIES TO FLOURISH

In Chapters 3 and 4, we looked at the community in the Old and New Testament. Both allowed for a variety of adults, not just parents, to have an input into teaching, talking, and sharing with children. However, parents are not completely "off the hook" in terms of their own responsibility, but they have help and support from others in fulfilling this task. We understand that parents who feel inadequate when instructing their children in spiritual matters should be helped by missional communities.

I am also drawn to the link between the Hebrew word for the household, *bet'ab* (the father's house) and missional communities. I can't help but feel that they play an important part in the fulfillment of a child's destiny. They can provide experiences of unconditional love, warmth, and acceptance from the tiniest baby up through all ages. Remember that communities in the Bible were places to experience the Father's blessing, care, and protection in an experience of a "team" (see Chapter 3). And they were not exclusive to just relatives; households in the Old Testament took in foreigners, orphans, and widows also.

In Chapter 4 we looked at *oikos*—extended households. It's as if God had set vehicles in place in the Old Testament that would be ready for accelerated growth in the New Testament. *Oikos* networks expanded and grew rapidly as people were radically reorientated toward Jesus who transformed their lives. I believe that missional communities should be considered in some shape or form as a way to direct our ministry to children, teenagers, and families back toward a biblical model that allows for intergenerational discipleship and supernatural mission.

I realize that each church is at a different place on the journey, using all manner of different leadership styles and structures; even so, I hope this account of one church's experience of missional communities can possibly spark something for you to consider whatever the size or type of your congregation.

Chapter Nine

WHAT IS TO COME

I hope and pray that this book will help you as an individual or as a church to biblically reflect on the status of children before God and the place they hold in the life of your faith community. Many leaders have asked me how they should go about writing and publicizing a vision for children and families in *their* church. I could just shrug my shoulders and tell them to pray and ask God—or suggest that they copy someone else's vision statement (but I don't!).

A vision is meant to be owned and experienced. I suggest there may be an uncomfortable personal cost in obtaining it. The Christian church is not a business that requires a corporate paper-pushing exercise and a file folder that says "vision statement written." We are the Bride of Christ, in a state of preparation for our Bridegroom's return. Each soul on this planet is precious, and Jesus Christ has paid the full price for their redemption. Asking God for a vision for any area of ministry means you're asking Him to show you what is on His heart for *your church's* situation at *this moment* in time.

Following are some guidelines I wrote to help establish a vision for children and family ministry, and which I've used to provide the baseline to work from in the two churches I've served.

CREATING A VISION FOR CHILDREN, YOUTH, AND FAMILY MINISTRY

The steps to implement a vision for children and young people in your church are to:

1. Get armed with information from culture and Christian research.

2. Become familiar with passages in the Bible pertaining to children and young people.

3. Develop an open heart and mind to be challenged and changed, stirred and broken.

The next step might not be needed; however, keep in mind that vision *for the future rises from the ashes of repentance.*

4. Repent for any wrong attitudes personally or corporately held toward children and young people (see Chapter 5).

5. Read, reflect, and become comfortable with the following definitions *before* proceeding to the next step.

> *Values*—principles held that informed the vision process.

> *Vision*—the place children's, youth, and all age ministry should go.

> *Process*—how the vision is to become reality

6. Write out your theological non-negotiables about children and young people. These are the values that are really important to you.

Following is an example of what I wrote for my last church:

Children start with God. However, they can easily "default" and veer away from Him if there is no twin strategy of evangelism and nurture. Every young person needs to hear the Good News and be nurtured in their faith journey.

Children and teenagers need to be given *regular* opportunities to personally respond to what God has done through Jesus' death and resurrection and to keep on saying "yes" to Jesus through "thick and thin," throughout their stages of cognitive and spiritual development.

Children and young people are capable of understanding their position in Christ, as precious, chosen people whose prayers are heard and who are worthy of the Father's love. They are "welcome at the table."

Children and young people are part of the Joel 2:28 promise: "I will pour out My Spirit on all flesh." We are not to construct a theology of "what is not for them." We uphold that there is no "junior" Holy Spirit.

7. Write out what, in your wildest dreams, you would like to see in the future. This is your *vision*.

Mine is tightly worded into three bullet points. Check your church's vision statement. Hopefully yours won't be going in the opposite direction!

Here is my example:

For children here to love God with all their heart, mind, and strength their whole lives long.

For children here to truly understand what it means to be God's child; to belong to Him; to occupy a special and unique place.

For children here to talk confidently with God, to listen to God with expectancy, to be overflowing with the Holy Spirit and know how to receive from Him, to say "yes" to God at every opportunity, and to advance the Kingdom for Him, living lives so that others see Jesus.

8. Think about how you are going to get there. What needs to change? This is the *process*.

Here is my example:

Maintain serious, targeted prayer, and obedience to whatever God says and with the Holy Spirit's help.

Outline and explain the values and vision above, in all leadership contexts—elders, staff, and missional community contexts.

For vision to become reality, seek opportunities to "teach the vision," establish leadership support, and demonstrate practical "modelling."

9. Finally, writing a vision requires the heart to follow it through to implementation. It needs to be presented to vestry, deacons, board members, and/or elders. It needs to be taught from the front. *It needs to underpin every leadership decision made.*

The vision needs to have people behind it who can make it happen, who are passionate about being totally reliant on God and passionate about the vision. Thus, the initial four steps are more important than anything else as they prepare the ground for what the Lord wants to plant in and through you.

BUILDING A TEAM

In my experience, building a team has not been hard. Communicating a vibrant vision is the most important factor in ensuring success, and I have had tremendous help from the senior leaders around me, in that they've let me live this out in all types of settings. Although we have not been perfect, we have aimed to teach, preach, and lead as a team. Honoring one another's gifting and skills has helped tremendously, as well as being secure in your own identity as a leader, so that you're not "grabbing the microphone" from another to give your area of ministry or particular interest additional airtime!

Ministry to children and young people is not just life-changing; it ensures the survival of the Church. Small, aging congregations are facing closure simply because there are no people being added. Whereas, young people can be very gifted at communicating the Good News with their peers and their families, and I believe have a role in growing the church. They are to be catalysts in seeing the Gospel spread through relational networks in these coming days.

I also believe in what Bill Hybels calls "the power of the ask."[134] Who is God earmarking to help you in the tasks ahead? I have found time after time when I have needed someone for a key role, when I was out of ideas and feeling exhausted, God brought someone right across my path—a midweek club leader, an administrative assistant, male leaders for a specific age-group, and summer cover teams. Sometimes the Lord provides for this supernaturally—I believe this is because the needs of children are on His heart.

One notable example involved the nursery at my last church. Volunteers were turning over quickly, and the nursery ministry leader had resigned. No one wanted to take the leadership position on. Realizing the great importance of the nursery team who show little ones what God is like (see Chapter 2), I had asked lots of people but to no avail. So, I went into the prayer room, lay down on the floor, and simply cried out to God on behalf of the little ones. I wrote down my dreams and visions and what was blocking these from happening. I asked God to move in this situation. This was around 11:00 in the morning.

That same afternoon, I got a call from two women who had met for prayer that very same morning and felt that they should offer to co-lead the nursery team. I was overjoyed as I knew God had "fixed it." I would not have asked them to lead because they had young babies themselves, and yet they were the right people and brought a period of stability and love to the nursery ministry at that time.

Volunteers are also slow to come forward into our areas of ministry if they are unclear about what is expected of them. You can help alleviate these concerns, though, by meeting prospective volunteers and talking through the responsibilities and expectations, and reviewing how they feel about their service at specific points. Do they have any training needs? How can you help with this? Obviously, with large numbers of volunteers, I must delegate some of these tasks to individual team leaders and encourage them to hold regular team meetings.

Training people appropriately, treating them with integrity, and genuinely thanking them and appreciating them are other keys to success. I have found over the years that a team is built on the foundations that the pastor, leader, or coordinator builds. If you start off on a "sandy place," it becomes much more difficult to shift the structure onto rock after it's been built.

REFRESHING THE TEAM

Perhaps you have a team in place but are experiencing high volunteer turnover. I am not writing the next few lines because I profess to be an expert on volunteer recruitment, nor do I want to take this book off in another direction. Rather, I want to end this book well by encouraging all of us to think about the value we place on the army of volunteers who assist us in the development and implementation of a new way of working with children, young people, and families. They are absolutely essential to us, and given that this book has been written to help us get ready for what is to come, we definitely will benefit from refreshing and renewing the hearts of volunteers who are already with us, as we're going to need more of them!

Vision Again!

I know I have stated this repeatedly, but it bears being repeated once again. When your volunteer team or congregation know exactly what they are working toward, they are less likely to become dry and burnt out. Vision isn't onerous; it actually brings refreshing in and of itself. I continue to watch my former church's journey[135] with great interest, as they seek to "call the city to life." Most of the congregation (including the children who were consulted too) can tell you what this vision seeks to do and the part they play in it.

Give Leaders Your Time

This sounds like stating the obvious, but in our increasingly busy lives, if we don't reply to texts, emails, or phone calls, volunteers feel undervalued. We all make mistakes and forget, so at least try to follow the 80/20 rule (get it right 80 percent of the time).

Listen, Listen, and Listen

Children's and youth leaders need your attention. Please remember that they might spend up to 50 or 75 percent of their time outside the main services. Pastors and leaders may tend to listen more to leaders of adult groups than to children's leaders. Think of the importance sometimes given to small group leaders or those on the mission field rather than to those who minister to the youngest. If children's leaders make suggestions to you, try not to take them as criticisms or disloyalty; if they are taking the time to talk to you, they obviously care and might genuinely see something that you haven't noticed. When team leaders have expressed their struggles to me regarding things that I have no control over, I still needed to make sure that I was listening carefully. Don't be defensive. This is easier to read here than it is to practice!

Ensure Your Team Receives Resources

Do any of your volunteers pay for craft supplies, for example, out of their own pocket? Can you do anything to rectify this? It's a rare volunteer who will do this year in and year out without feeling a little bit aggrieved. I'd suggest it's not honoring to the person or the ministry to assume they will cover the cost automatically just because no one asks them about it or addresses the situation.

Arrange Regular Training

Obviously, the churches that I have been part of have been able to provide the cost for the training I have received and then passed on to my teams. What of those of us who are in smaller churches who might not have the funds to provide training? Can you perhaps join with others and host a training day together? As a personal example, I began to open up my annual Vision and Training Day in this way; recently, we have had eight denominations present and over twenty churches represented.

Reduce Meetings

Instead of scheduling another monthly evening meeting, be prepared to talk with individuals on Sunday mornings or help set up and/or chat informally at the end of a class, without resorting to "meeting upon meeting." Release leaders to be the best at what they do. Staff members need to remember that volunteers are just that—volunteers. They have a life outside of what they do in our churches!

Show Appreciation

Consider hosting thank-you events or socials for your children and youth leaders. Have a pizza night, or schedule a bowling trip. Don't allow your volunteers to pay! Ask for donations from other people in your fellowship or submit the costs through your budget, if you are able to do so.

Give Updates to Your Church

Ensure that the entire church hears reports of what is happening in the children's and youth ministry. Celebrate successes of your team(s). Pray for the kids and youth leaders in services—not just at holiday club time.

Consider the Use of Language

Is our language inclusive of everyone in all services and meetings? Does it come across that we value the work that is done with children and young people? How do your volunteers feel if they hear that "our worship will begin once the young people have left for their own groups"?

Verbally Thank Your Volunteers

Verbally thank your volunteers often and go out of your way to pass on encouragement. This sounds so obvious, and yet we can be so poor at doing it. Unfortunately, we are often quicker to pass on complaints or criticisms than compliments.

Pray with and for Your Volunteers

Valuable moments are made for volunteer teams when the senior pastor or another pastor prays personally for them—in whatever way you are comfortable, but in some *demonstrable* way that expresses your desire for them to be filled with the knowledge of God.

Provide Opportunities to Encounter God

Give your volunteers opportunities to encounter God—Father, Son, and Holy Spirit—in an experiential and tangible way. I have an unscientific theory that postulates that volunteers in children and youth ministry quit sooner than those in worship bands or small group leadership. I really do think we pay less attention to those serving behind the scenes, doing what may be construed as "less important work" with the youngest ones amongst us.

So rather than have a chip on my shoulder, my response is: *what can I do to allow these precious people to have the best experience possible? To help them grow and be affirmed?* I want my teams to know what has lifted me up when I hit rock bottom, wishing I'd been called to the ministry of coffee-making! *It's the power and presence of God*—His absolute approval for us because we're His children, no matter what we do or how we do it.

Minister the tender-heartedness of God the Father to your team. Teach on the priestly role that Jesus occupies for them now. Welcome the power of the Holy Spirit to move amongst you as you gather your volunteers together for prayer, for teaching, or for a meal. It's not good to serve in any ministry without the infilling of the Holy Spirit. Put simply, we run dry. Teach volunteers about the *phileo* love God has for each of His children—the demonstrated, natural affection of the Father which He wants to lavish on each one of us (see 1 John 3:1).

PARTNERSHIP WITH PARENTS

Parents require gentle and skillful care and significant understanding and compassion. We parents can sometimes feel very fragile. At times we attempt to live our lives vicariously through our children. In other matters, we are sensitive to the ways we have been hurt in the past which may influence our own children's experience of life and faith. There is not a parent who doesn't need the faith community's help to keep doing what they do. Parents value pastoral care and compassion from the children and youth ministry team (or from their missional community/house group) more than a vast program of events. Relationship is much more important than programs or activities.

On a practical level, parents greatly appreciate communication, whether it be in person or by email or by texting. (And don't assume that teenagers pass information on to parents!) We all realize that family life continues to be so complex and busy in terms of of regular and extra-curricular activity commitments.

And parents need to be loved and accepted. They should not be treated or considered as just the provider of the fodder in the children's and youth groups, or the contributors to staff salaries. They are valuable and dearly loved. I enjoy spending time with them and encouraging them. They play a very important part in constructing the future history of every young person they raise. I enjoy helping them to think of ways to be missional as a family and to look for the networks God is leading each of them into as well the witness they have as a family together.

Truly I believe that we are on the cusp of an increasing impact into the world in which we live and work—to see the reorientation of whole households as it was so long ago.

My conclusion is that this impact can happen only when the church partners fully with the work of the Father, Son, and Holy Spirit. Gone are the days of choosing to emphasize one more than the other Persons of the Trinity. It is through the rest which the Father gives that we learn our true value and worth, that leads us to do the works of the Son in the power of the Holy Spirit.

LOOKING TO THE FUTURE

Nothing makes me more excited than to consider what is ahead for us. My heart overflows with hope when I read Psalm 78:4-7:

> *We will not hide* [things we have heard]
> *from their descendants;*
> *we will tell the next generation*
> *the praiseworthy deeds of the Lord,*
> *His power, and the wonders He has done.*
> *He decreed statutes for Jacob*
> *and established the law in Israel,*
> *which He commanded our ancestors*
> *to teach their children,*
> *so the next generation would know them,*

even the children yet to be born,
and they in turn would tell their children.
Then they would put their trust in God
and would not forget His deeds
but would keep His commands.

I started this book by saying that it was outside the scope of this project to cover the details of how to run successful children, youth, and family ministries. There are many brilliant "how-to" books. Instead, I wanted to write something that would bridge the gap between the world of ministry to young people and the rest of the church! I wanted to excite and challenge you as leaders, pastors, ministers, parents, and children's workers *for that which is ahead.*

In April 2011, a fellow leader asked me what I thought was needed to happen to fully allow a wind of change to sweep through many of our churches. He referred to Second Kings 3, verses 15b-20 (NKJV):

Then it happened, when the musician played, that the hand of the Lord came upon [Elisha]. *And he said, "Thus says the Lord: 'Make this valley full of ditches.' For thus says the Lord: 'You shall not see wind, nor shall you see rain; yet that valley shall be filled with water, so that you, your cattle, and your animals may drink.' And this is a simple matter in the sight of the Lord; He will also deliver the Moabites into your hand. Also you shall attack every fortified city and every choice city, and shall cut down every good tree, and stop up every spring of water, and ruin every good piece of land with stones." Now it happened in the morning, when the grain offering was offered, that suddenly water came by way of Edom,* **and the land was** **filled with water.**

Here, I have used the New King James Version, and you can also read a similar translation in The Message. It's important to note that somehow the valley was able to hold water; some kind of structural change happened to the sides of the valley to contain the water. I am a former teacher of geography, and I understand that valleys don't retain water; rather, water flows through them, and they continue to be "carved" by the downward movement of the water on its journey to a lake or the sea. So...something miraculous happened overnight!

It is time to get the ditches ready—to prepare the structures for what is ahead! I believe we will see again the transformation of society that is inextricably linked to the transformation of family life. Children will lead their parents and vice versa. We are in desperate need of advice and guidance on how to nurture children's spirituality and not to ignore or destroy it, in order that these young ones would go further than we have ever gone before. Speaking as one who is based in the United Kingdom, we are in desperate need of any intervention from God that will stop the decline of children and young people from our churches.

I hope I have explained that continual separation and compartmentalizing may not be the best model for whole-life missional discipleship, even though good things may happen to each group. Yet…let's not keep the status quo—let's go from good to great!

I realize that I have written a lot about my experiences in a larger setting. So if you attend or pastor a smaller church, I want to highlight that the *principles* within this book can be applied anywhere. In fact, larger churches might find it more difficult to practice intergenerational interaction well. Smaller can sometimes mean lighter structures, with a greater ability to respond to change and mix the ages with less difficulty. I hope that the point of this book—to prepare for a spiritual awakening—may encourage and stimulate your planning and thinking.

I know that not all of what I say and write is popular. Much of it is uncomfortable, and it might look messy. I have challenged you to look closely at your church's vision and purpose and analyze the way children and young people are viewed. I believe I have been faithful to what He has asked me to do. In a time of prayer and meditation in August 2009, I wrote specifically what I felt the Lord was saying:

> You will, and already have, encountered great opposition, even from those who carry a revivalist anointing, because partitions equal comfort. Partitions mean each need can be catered for comfortably. There is a time and a place for this, but in these days, dismantling is necessary as I want to teach the revivalists that great power is exhibited by the weak, the small, the inexperienced, and the young. Adults will walk in even greater power when they partner with the young.

Three years later, I found myself reading Keith White on children and the Kingdom (mentioned in Chapter 7). Jesus, the little child placed in the midst, and the kingdom of Heaven are a triad—three closely related persons or entities. In music, a triad represents notes that come together in harmony as a chord. Keith White suggests that:

> Each part of the triad illuminates the other two; to attack or marginalize one is to despise the other two; in welcoming or receiving one, the other two are also accepted."[136]

This has major implications in our church's understanding and treatment of children. I sense that it might mean that what God was impressing on me was true: *Adults will walk in even greater power when they partner with the young.*

Does this mean that we will gain a greater understanding and experience of the Kingdom of God, when we are in a right understanding of the relationship between children, Jesus, and the Kingdom? We have seen how the Greek text states that the Kingdom of God is children's—literally *"belonging to such as these is the kingdom of God."* (See Chapter 1.)

As adults, we will always (quite rightly) spend some time apart from children, doing age-specific activities. I sense, however, a renewed urgency to really press in to demonstrate the same heart that Jesus had toward the young. *Perhaps we will not see the harvest we long for, until we nurture the gift that has already been given to the Church—the young. Perhaps then we will see the Kingdom released through us all in greater measure.* Heaven knows our world needs it. Might children be the catalyst to bring in the harvest of not-yet believing parents and extended household members?

Heavenly Father, may it be so.

ENDNOTES

1. Dorling Kindersley research cited on July 19, 2007, in *The Times/Sunday Times*. Available online at http://www.timesonline.co.uk.

2. Hugh Black, *Revival: Including the Prophetic Vision Of Jean Darnall* (Greenock, Scotland: New Dawn Books, 1993). Excerpt available online at http://www.crossrhythms.co.uk/propheticwords/jeandarnalls vision.

3. Rebecca Nye, *Children's Spirituality* (London, England: Church House Publishing, 2009), 5.

4. Ibid., 9.

5. Michael Brooks, "Natural Born Believers," *New Scientist* (February 7, 2009): 30-33.

6. Nye, 41-70. Note the acrostic SPIRIT, standing for Space, Process, Imagination, Relationship, Intimacy, and Trust.

7. Ron Buckland, *Children and God* (London, England: Scripture Union, 1988) 27ff.

8. Martha Ellen Stortz, "'Where or When Was Your Servant Innocent?' Augustine on Childhood," in *The Child in Christian Thought*, ed. Marcia Bunge (Grand Rapids, MI: Eerdmans, 2001), 79.

9. Buckland, 33.

10. Urie Bronfenbrenner, *The Ecology of Human Development* (Cambridge, MA; London, England: Harvard UP, 1979), 285.

11. Margaret Bendroth, "Horace Bushnell's *Christian Nurture*," *The Child in Christian Thought*, 356.

12. Buckland, 42.

13. Ibid, 45.

14. Roy Zuck, *Precious in His Sight* (Grand Rapids, MI: Baker Books, 1997), 206.

15. Judith M. Gundry, "Children in the Gospel of Mark," in *The Child in the Bible*, eds. Marcia Bunge, Terrence Fretheim (Grand Rapids, MI: Eerdmans, 2008), 151.

16. C.E.B. Cranfield, *The Gospel According to Saint Mark* (Cambridge, England: Cambridge University Press, 1959), 32.

17. Gundry, 151.

18. Mariella Frostrup, "Life & Style" column, *Observer Newspaper Magazine* (January 15, 2012): 54. Available online at http://www.guardian.co.uk/lifeandstyle/2012/jan/15/mariella -frostrup-mother-frustrated-church.

19. Wanderlust Productions, *Finger of God* DVD, 2007. Further information on how to obtain this from http://wanderlustproductions.net.

20. See http://www.lynnalexander.org.uk.

21. Available online at http://www.lausanne.org/docs/2004forum/LOP47_IG18.pdf.

22. Ted Ward's *Foreword* in J. Wilhoit & J. Dettoni, *Nurture That Is Christian* (Grand Rapids, MI: Baker Books, 1995), 9.

23. John Westerhoff, *Will Our Children Have Faith?* (rev. ed.), (Toronto, ON: Morehouse Publishing, 2000), xii.

24. Ibid., 36.

25. Ibid., 92.

26. Ibid., 94.

27. Ibid., 88.

28. Banning Liebscher posted this on Twitter, June 3, 2011 (permission obtained to use quote).

29. Wark-Clements Productions, *LA Mix*, television program broadcast in 1996.

30. Gordon Wenham, "Family in the Pentateuch," in *Family in the Bible*, R. Hess and M.D. Carroll, eds. (Grand Rapids, MI: Baker Books, 2003), 21.

31. Daphne Kirk, *Reconnecting the Generations* (Buxhall, England: Kevin Mayhew, 2001), 9-10.

32. Strong's #1755.

33. John and Paula Sandford, *Restoring the Christian Family* (Tulsa, OK: Victory House Publishing, 1979), 21.

34. For example: Neil Anderson, *Steps to Freedom in Christ* (London, England: Monarch Books, 2003).

35. Wenham, 21.

36. Sandford, 24.

37. Cynthia Jones Neal, "The Power of Vygotsky," in *Nurture That Is Christian*, 124.

38. Bronfenbrenner, 3.

39. Neil, 127.

40. Ibid.

41. Santiago Guijarro, "The Family in First-Century Galilee," in *Constructing Early Christian Families*, Halvor Moxnes, ed. (London, England: Routledge, 1997), 46.

42. Halvor Moxnes, 23.

43. Rodney Stark, *The Rise of Christianity* (San Francisco, CA: HarperSanFrancisco, 1997), 3.

44. Ibid., 6,12.

45. Ibid., 10.

46. Ibid., 16.

47. Nicky Gumbel, *How to Revolutionise Your Relationships* (London, England: Alpha International, 2008), 9.

48. Stark, 115-117.

49. A.E.R. Boak, "A History of Rome to 565 A.D." in R. Stark, 116.

50. Excavated from the port city of Ashkelon by Lawrence E. Stager in 1991. A full report of this is in *Biblical Archaeology Review* 17, 34-53.

51. Plato, *Laws* 7.808d, in *Children in the Early Church*, ed. W.A. Strange (Carlisle, England: Paternoster Press, 1996), 6.

52. Philo, *De Opificio Mundi*, 165, in W.A. Strange, 15.

53. Ibid., 19.

54. Joel B. Green, "'Tell Me a Story': Perspectives on Children from the Acts of the Apostles," in *The Child in the Bible*, 222.

55. Mike Breen and Alex Absalom, *Launching Missional Communities: A Field Guide* (Pawleys Island, SC: 3DM, 2010), 33-37.

56. Ibid., 35.

57. James Dunn, "Romans 9–16," in Breen and Absalom, 35.

58. Eusebius, "Martyrdom of Polycarp 9.3," in *A New Eusebius: Documents Illustrating the History of the Church to AD 337*, eds. J. Stevenson, W.H.C. Frend (London, England: SPCK, 1987), 25.

59. Justin Martyr, *The First Apology 1.15*, in *Children in the Early Church*, 83.

60. Cicero, *On Duties 1, 53-5*, in *The Roman Household: A Sourcebook*, eds. Jane F. Gardner, Thomas Wiedemann (London, England: Routledge, 1991), 2.

61. Green, "Tell Me a Story," *The Child in the Bible*, 229.

62. Dennis L. Stamps, "Children in Late Antiquity," in *Dictionary of New Testament Background*, eds. C.A. Evans, S.E. Porter (Downers Grove, IL: IVP Academic, 2000), 200-1.

63. Strange, 74.

64. Pliny, *Letter 10.96.9*, in *A New Eusebius*, 19.

65. Green, "Tell Me a Story," *The Child in the Bible*, 231.

66. Available online at http://www.4to14window.com.

67. At the "Reaching Children" forum, Streamwood, Illinois, April 5-6, 2009. Attended by 94 leaders from 54 organizations.

68. Mike Booker and Mark Ireland, *Evangelism—Which Way Now?* (London, England: Church House Publishing, 2003), 110.

69. David Martyn Lloyd-Jones, *Preaching and Preachers* (Grand Rapids, MI: Zondervan, 1972), 128.

70. Available online at http://www.charismamag.com/index.php/blogs/rtkendall/22

209-judging-is-gods-prerogative;
see also R.T. Kendall, *Total Forgiveness* (London, England: Hachette UK, 2010).

71. Fully detailed in Jerome Berryman, *Godly Play* (Minneapolis, MN: Augsburg Fortress, 1999).

72. Sophia Cavalletti, *The Religious Potential of the Child* (Chicago, IL: Liturgy Training Publications, 1992), 138-139.

73. Found in several "Famous Quotes" websites, but there is agreement that the original source cannot be located, and as such, this quote has been described as a form of poetry rather than scientific research.

74. Judith Gundry, "To Such As These Belongs the Reign of God: Jesus and Children," *Theology Today* (January 2000): 479–480.

75. Available online at
     http://www.lausanne.org,
     in the *Documents* section of the website (Occasional Paper 47).

76. Peter Brierley, *Religious Trends 7, 2007/08* (Swindon, England: Christian Research, 2007), 12.2.

77. Ibid.

78. Ibid.

79. See http://www.theamericanchurch.org for details of the research project.

80. During a presentation entitled, "Spirituality Through the Eyes of a Child" in Glasgow, UK, in March 2011.

81. See http://www.wymad.org.uk for further information. This is an online collaboration of agencies under the banner of "Will You Make A Difference?" (WYMAD).

82. See http://www.4to14window.comfor further information. Online resources are available to support this initiative to join Christians from all denominations together to see young people ages 4 to 14 reached with the Good News.

83. Further comprehensive information is available online at http://www.barna.org. I particularly recommend subscribing to the email updates. Subscribers are never over-mailed, and the updates are always succinct and thought-provoking.

84. Larry Richards, *A Theology of Children's Ministry* (Grand Rapids, MI: Zondervan, 1983), in the denominational booklet, "Children, Church and God: Some Baptist Perspectives" (Glasgow, Scotland: Baptist Union of Scotland, 2005), 19.

85. Two very helpful resources: D. Kirk, *When a Child Asks to Be Baptized* and *When a Child Asks to Take Communion* (both Stowmarket, England: Kevin Mayhew, 1999). Possibly out of print and best obtained from http://www.daphnekirk.org.

86. Punishments: such as parents and employers refusing to supply the child/adult with food and drink and even banishment from the country. See Strohl, "The Child in Luther's Theology," *The Child in Christian Thought*, 146.

87. An event I ran in my local church, which has now developed into a national event in Scotland in partnership with Scripture Union. Further information available online at http://www.suscotland.org.uk/pray/pray-any-way.aspx or by contacting S.U. Scotland directly.

88. Further information available online at http://www.celluk.org.uk or by contacting the Cell Church movement directly.

89. Formerly Cell Church Solutions (CCS). See particularly www.joelcomiskeygroup.com/articles/basics/familyVsGender.htm.

90. As of December 2011.

91. Steven Anderson and James Renwick, *Life to the Full: Essentials for Following Jesus* (Glasgow, Scotland: Healing Rooms Scotland, 2011). Available from www.healingrooms-scotland.com.

92. Available from http://www.daphnekirk.org.

93. Graeme C. Young, *Luke Into Jesus* (Maitland, FL: Xulon press, 2011).

94. George Barna, *Transforming Children into Spiritual Champions* (Ventura, CA: Regal Books, 2003), 78.

95. For examples of radical evangelistic and discipleship activity by children as young as eight, see O. Goldenberg, *The Joshua Generation* (Maidstone, Kent: River Publishing, 2011).

96. Barna, 105.

97. George Barna quote from *The Barna Leadership Seminar Volume 1* DVD teaching resource (stand-alone sessions suitable for

churches, parents, ministry leaders) available from Christian booksellers, and available online from http://www.barna.org. See also George Barna, *Think Like Jesus* (Nashville, TN: Thomas Nelson, 2003).

98. The Barna Organization DVD already mentioned provides a stand-alone teaching resource that can be watched and discussed with your church family.

99. The respondents were asked about personal faith, assurance, and Heaven; and based on these responses, they were described as "born again."

100. Keith J. White, "'He Placed a Little Child in the Midst': Jesus, the Kingdom, and Children," *The Child in the Bible*, 356.

101. Rev. Ashley Collishaw, quoted with permission, in a private email to the author.

102. Ivy Beckwith, *Postmodern Children's Ministry* (Grand Rapids, MI: Zondervan, 2004) 31.

103. Heidi Baker, *Always Enough: God's Miraculous Provision Among the Poorest Children on Earth* (Grand Rapids, MI: Chosen Books, 2003).

104. Luke 2:49.

105. Westerhoff, 90.

106. Ronald Kydd, *Charismatic Gifts in the Early Church: An Exploration into the Gifts of the Spirit During the First Three Centuries of the Christian Church* (Peabody, MA: Hendrickson Publishers, 1991), 87.

107. Ibid.

108. Harry Sprange, *Children in Revival* (Fearn, Scotland: Christian Focus Publications, 2002), 37.

109. Kenneth J. Hardman, *Issues in American Christianity, Primary Sources with Introductions* (Grand Rapids, MI: Baker Books, 1993), 120.

110. David Kinnaman, *You Lost Me: Why Young People are Leaving Church and Rethinking Faith* (Grand Rapids, MI: Baker Books, 2011), 115.

111. Ibid.

112. Gordon Fee and Douglas Stewart, *How to Read the Bible for All Its Worth* (Grand Rapids, MI: Zondervan, 2003) is a great one to start with.

113. I find this a very practical and informative book: Ben Quash and Michael Ward, eds., *Heresies and How To Avoid Them* (London, England: SPCK, 2007), or in the United States (Peabody, MA: Hendrickson Publishers, 2007).

114. This is a reference to John Stott and N.T. (Tom) Wright, both renowned scholars and eminently readable.

115. George Barna quote from *The Barna Leadership Seminar Volume 1* DVD teaching resource.

116. Kinnaman, 116

117. John and Chris Leach, *And For Your Children* (Crowborough, East Sussex: Monarch, 1994), 59.

118. Please see http://uk.24-7prayer.com/prayer-rooms/. You will be inspired and moved—read about all ages taking part! Prayer rooms are held in schools, churches, homes, community centers— you can set up a prayer room anywhere.

119. Stormie Omartian, *The Power of the Praying Kid* (Eugene, OR: Harvest House Publishers, 2005).

120. Matt Redman, lyrics for "Mission's Flame" (*Facedown* album).

121. Toronto Airport Christian Fellowship, now known as Catch the Fire Toronto.

122. I love that this is prominently posted in huge lettering on the walls of the Airport campus.

123. Soaking prayer is the practice of quietening oneself, being still and resting in God, and thinking or meditating about God and His Word. It can be done in total silence or with gentle music playing, alone or with others, the point being that one focuses solely on God. There is no emptying of the mind or seeking spiritual guides; it is simply time to fix eyes on Jesus (see Heb. 12:2), talk to and listen to God, and allow Him to pour His love and peace out into our hearts. Occasionally, we may pray for people as they soak or rest in God's presence, but this involves very little or no spoken words so that we do not interrupt their time of communing (being) with God. *I find that children manage this*

easily for short periods of time, once they have been taught how and why. They love to be quiet with Father God.

124. Booker and Ireland, 162.

125. See http://www.kkint.net for further information.

126. One of these courses was filmed for the 2008 Alpha Invitation DVD. It captured the warm messiness of adults and children half-filling a large hall over a substantial meal prepared by our amazing chef, Gillian.

127. These can be purchased at https://shop.alpha.org/.

128. See Mike Breen's 3DM organization, www.weare3DM.com (US based but with worldwide influence). Also www.3dmuk.com. In the UK, see http://www.missionalcommunities.co.uk—the highly acclaimed Missional Communities Field Guide is available here.

129. See http://www.stthomaschurch.org.uk.

130. Text available online at Mike's blog— http://mikebreen.wordpress.com/2011/09/12/why-the-missional-movement-will-fail.

131. Breen and Absalom, 18.

132. Stark, 16.

133. Mike Breen and S. Cockram, *Building a Discipling Culture* (Pawleys Island, SC: 3DM, 2009), 7.

134. Bill Hybels, *The Volunteer Revolution: Unleashing the Power of Everybody* (Grand Rapids, MI: Zondervan, 2004), 105. This is an excellent book for paid staff who harness volunteer power.

135. Queens Park Baptist Church, Glasgow, further information available on http://www.qpbc.org.

136. Keith White, "He Placed a Little Child in the Midst," *The Child in the Bible*, 356.

CONTACT THE AUTHOR

Tweet your thoughts to @lynnos

Website:
www.lynnalexander.org.uk

Additional copies of this book and other book
titles from EVANGELISTA MEDIA™
and DESTINY IMAGE™ EUROPE
are available at your local bookstore.

We are adding new titles every month!

To view our complete catalog online, visit us at:
www.evangelistamedia.com

Send a request for a catalog to:

**Via della Scafa, 29/14
65013 Città Sant'Angelo (Pe), ITALY
Tel. +39 085 4716623 • Fax +39 085 9090113
info@evangelistamedia.com**

"Changing the World, One Book at a Time."

Are you an author?
Do you have a "today" God-given message?

CONTACT US

We will be happy to review your manuscript
for the possibility of publication:

publisher@evangelistamedia.com
http://www.evangelistamedia.com/pages/AuthorsAppForm.htm